Loneliness: The Untapped Resource

LONELINESS:
The Untapped Resource

Ida Nelle Hollaway

BROADMAN PRESS
Nashville, Tennessee

Verses marked KJV are from the King James Version of the
Bible.

Verses marked RSV are from the Revised Standard Version of
the Bible, copyrighted 1946, 1952, © 1971, 1973.

Verses marked Moffatt are from *The Bible: a New Translation* by
James A. R. Moffatt. Copyright © 1935 by Harper and Row, Pub-
lishers, Inc. Used by permission.

Dewey Decimal Classification: 152.4
Subject heading: LONELINESS
Library of Congress Catalog Card Number: 81-66557
Printed in the United States of America

Contents

1
The Universal Pain

It is after midnight, and the room is dark and still. Four-year-old Robbie awakens to sights which look unfamiliar to him. Objects and shadows take on fiendish shapes. The wind blows a shrub against the window, and he wonders if the scratching sound it makes is someone trying to pull the screen away. Robbie's mouth is dry, and sound will hardly come from it. The tiny cry he finally manages falls on sleeping ears in the bedroom down the hall. A new fear grips him. Maybe his parents aren't even home. Maybe they have had to go away somewhere and have left him by himself. He pulls the covers around him more tightly. He feels so small, so frightened, and so lonely.

Lynn sits looking at the new workbooks her father has bought tonight for her classes at Maplewood Elementary. They are a different series from the ones she has been using at Dale Hollow before they had to move. She looks more closely at the math book and feels a rush of panic. Multiplication tables on the first few pages? She hasn't had any multiplication tables yet! Why do schools have to be so different?

She almost cries when she thinks of the first day she has just spent at the new school. Her parents had

warned her that it might be "open space," but she had
not had any idea what that meant. She had never seen
inside a classroom where you didn't even have a desk of
your own. When you had a desk, at least you knew
where you belonged!

Lynn had been confused all day. Once she got the
nerve to slip up to a friendly looking boy to ask him
where to go, but before she could speak he blurted out,
"What's the matter, four eyes? Are you lost?"

Several of the children laughed. It was the first time
Lynn had noticed that she was the only child in the
room with glasses. Ede, her best friend, had worn them
at Dale Hollow and so had Michael, the smartest boy in
the room.

No one had taken the trouble to explain the schedule
to her, but she soon learned not to ask questions. She
had asked one of the girls when dinner would be.

"Hey, everybody!" the girl had called out. "Get a load
of this! The Southern belle wants to know when 'din-
nah is suhved.' "

"We call it lunch, friend," another girl answered.
"It's at 11:45."

They had called it "the dinner hour" at Dale Hollow.

A tear slipped down Lynn's cheek as she looked at
the new workbooks. Everything was so different. The
books were different. The rooms were different. Most
of all, the kids were different. They had never made fun
of her at Dale Hollow. She had lots of friends there.

The tears came faster now. She felt so confused, so
far away from her friends, so very lonely.

Lisa has hurried home from her high school as quickly as she could. She slipped in the back door and hurried

to her own bedroom and locked the door. She is lying on her bed trying to hide her sobs in a pillow. She doesn't want to talk to anyone. She feels so humiliated, so disappointed, so absolutely awful. All spring, she and her friends have been planning the big prom. She has helped with the plans, with the fund raising, and with the decorations. She has whispered and giggled with the other girls for weeks as they have tried to decide which boy would probably invite which girl. Sometimes they have whispered in awe and dread of the possibility that someone would not be invited. They have assured each other that this could not possibly happen . . . not to one of them. After all, there were more boys than girls in the class, and they are the best known girls in school.

But it has happened. The prom is tomorrow night, and only Lisa has not been invited. All of her friends have already had calls about their corsages. Some of them have teased her today because they are so sure she is holding out on them, not telling who has invited her. How can she ever face them again when they find out? She can't bear the thought of all of them feeling sorry for her. It is the first time she ever remembers feeling so rejected, so much a failure, so terribly alone.

It is that time of evening when the college dorm seems almost deserted. Many of the students have hurried to the library or the ball game, or to one of the night classes. Others are strolling across the campus, hand in hand, or standing in the shadows of the giant trees.

Bill is standing by his dorm window looking out across the campus, shrouded by the night air. A distant shout and returning laugh just add to his feeling of iso-

lation. He sits down with a feeling that he is smothering. The walls of the small room seem to be caving in on him, trapping him. He stares out the window of the seventh floor room in the men's high rise. It seems to offer him an invitation to end his misery in one quick jump. He has checked out the drop from the window several times in the last few days. The drop to the concrete drive below is uncluttered, if he could only be sure that a dive from that window would really end his misery.

He has made few friends here, none who are especially close. He has worked hard, but his grades aren't measuring up to his family's expectations. They certainly aren't good enough to get the graduate grant they had planned on. How can he tell them? How could he expect them to understand? Life is so hard . . . and so alone.

David and Jeanne sit across from each other in the hospital waiting room. They look at each other, and there is pain and sorrow and fear in the eyes of each of them. But somehow they do not move closer together or make any attempt to touch, or to try to share the torture they feel. Their only son, Brett, is in the operating room beyond the closed doors. In one unguarded moment he had dashed out with exuberance to greet his dad as David had stepped off the bus across the street. The oncoming motorist could not stop in time. The small, mangled body bore its most serious wounds in the little skull. The doctors had been amazed he was still breathing. They offered scant hope that he could be saved. They only promised to do their best.

David and Jeanne sit in their own small worlds of isolation. Each relives the last hour over and over. Brett *had stood on that corner so many, many times and waited for his Dad. What was different about tonight? What had caused him to feel such urgency that he had forgotten all their past warnings? They feel so strongly the aloneness of their son as he walks through this struggle with death, knowing there is no way they can reach him, and nothing they can do to help him win this crucial battle. Each feels very alone in his own turmoil and sorrow. Suffering is such a lonely road.*

Cheryl is still feeling stunned, but enough of the numbness is wearing off to allow the intensity of the pain to beat against her head. All of the unanswered questions have blared out in her brain through the long night.

How could such a thing happen? Why had she not known? What were the signs she had missed? How had she failed so miserably? Could twenty-five years of marriage just be put aside?

Don had been out of town on a business trip for three days. She had gone to the market to get his favorite foods for a welcome-home meal. She wasn't sure why they had seemed a little less close of late. Perhaps, she had thought, if she dressed very carefully, had the house well cleaned, prepared a super dinner, let the kids eat out so they could be alone, things would surely improve.

Then she had come back from the market to find Don already there. He was making no effort to unpack.

"I'm not staying," he had said. "I can't live here any more. I don't love you, Cheryl. I haven't for some time now. I can't just keep on pretending. I'm getting a divorce."

Cheryl felt as if all the life had drained out of her.

Surely this was some terrible nightmare. All of the thousands of questions that would come to her mind later would not form now. She just stood there looking at Don in disbelief. Suddenly, she felt very small, like a child who was lost and bewildered.

Through the night she had fought the pain, the questions. Now she sat on the side of the bed staring at the empty, unrumpled side. It was morning, and a new day must be faced. There was much to do. Somehow, the children must be told. The flimsy excuse she gave last night must be denied. In all of her life she had never felt so completely alone in the world.

George had promised Ruth he would not react this way. They had known for some time that the end was inevitable. Their fifty-two years together had been wonderful. They had talked many times these last seven months of the joy they had known.

"I want to keep it that way," Ruth had said over and over. "I want you to remember me smiling and happy. I want you to stay happy too."

He had promised her that he would do just that.

"There's so much that still needs doin' in this old world," he had told her. "I'm sure I can always find someone to help, and helping others has always kept the two of us smilin'."

He had meant it when he had said it. He had really thought he could do it. He had not known it would be like this. It was all he could do to make himself get out of bed in the morning. Every day was the same. No Ruth to talk to over his coffee. It was no fun to putter around fixing breakfast any more. No one to share the morning paper. No one to plan little surprises for when he *walked to the grocery. It was as if the best part of himself had died with her.*

George's hands trembled as he watered her plants. At one moment he wished they would die so they wouldn't remind him of her so constantly; the next moment he thought he could not possibly bear it if they, too, were to die.

Fifty-two years they had walked together! He had forgotten what it was like to be alone . . . so very alone, and so lonely.

One night recently I was thinking of all these people . . . Robbie, Lynn, Lisa, Bill, David and Jeanne, Cheryl, and George. I was thinking how they represented the whole spectrum of life from the small child awake in the darkness to the weary old man who was learning to walk on alone. Yet they all had one thing in common. They shared a desperate loneliness. I was reminding myself that this pain knows no age barriers. All people of all ages are faced with it.

Even as I was thinking this, a news special came on that made me acutely aware of another phase of loneliness.

I was caught up in the look of agony on the face of the little girl on my television screen. The wild, staring eyes seemed to be too involved in a deeper suffering to even notice the large flies crawling over her nose and her tiny, drawn mouth. Only the bloated, distended stomach stood out in contrast to the thinly covered bones of the frail, little body. She was lying alone on the side of a dusty road.

Perhaps her parents had already died or were among those fallen, listless ones who seemed too near eternity to care or notice any longer what was happening about them. The only movement the camera caught was the twitching of the tiny hands of the little girl that seemed to be trying to reach out to someone or something. A pain gripped my own body as I sensed how utterly alone she must feel, as she lay dying. The news story passed on to another picture, another land, other views of human misery, but the face of that small girl dying alone is with me yet.

Only a few days before I had been talking with a group of six-year-olds about the word *alone*, and what it meant to them. "Afraid. Sad. Left out. All by yourself," were the answers they gave. But Shonda's answer was different. She didn't say anything at all for a while. Then she finally said in a near whisper, "Dark, bloody, and real, real, scared." The other children didn't ask any questions, and Shonda didn't volunteer anything further.

When they were gone I asked her if she would like to tell me more about her thoughts.

"Oh, I've been alone a lot," she said. "But the most alonest, scariest time of all was the night my mamma killed my daddy. See, he had been gone a long time, and my mamma had my little brother with a different daddy. Then *my* daddy came back, and he wanted my mamma. I guess he was drunk or somethin' cause he started trying to tear her clothes off, and she shot him and killed him. Then the ambulance came and got my daddy, and the police came and got my mother. I heard my little baby brother cryin' back in the bedroom, and so I ran back there to try to help him.

"Then everything got quiet, and I looked back in the livin' room, and nobody was there no more. They forgot

all about us. It was dark, and there was blood every-
where, and the baby was cryin' again. I screamed, and I
screamed, but nobody came. That was the scariest,
lonesomest time I was talkin' about."

"How old were you then, Shonda?" I asked her.

"I guess I was three or just turnin' four, cause you
see my little sister was born before I was five."

My heart ached for her, but it was not an unusual
sensation. In the last decade and a half of teaching
young children, I have felt a growing concern for the
amount of loneliness I encounter among them.

As I have traveled across our country speaking and
holding conferences related to my previous books on
depression, missions, and child guidance, I have en-
countered an increasing number of people of all ages
who are tormented by the growing problem of loneliness. As a result I have done an extensive study of what
is being written, especially by psychologists and sociologists, about this problem. In light of the examples I
have just given, I would like to point out some of the life
situations and personality factors which help to bring
on the pain of loneliness at the various stages of life.

The Young Child

Loneliness for the young child often begins with the
birth trauma itself. Many have come to agree on the
possible future effect of this sudden and radical separation from the very protective and all-providing environment of the mother's womb. It was the opinion of
the noted psychologist Otto Rank (in *The Trauma of
Birth*) that this trauma may well "set the universal tone
of the primal terror for all succeeding separations."

Many psychologists remind us that of all the troubles

that young children face, the effects of loneliness linger
with them the longest. The dread of not being loved or
wanted which grows out of parental conflicts, separations, and divorce is probably the most frequent cause.

It is certainly true that few experiences facing adults
are so traumatic, or so fraught with loneliness, as that
which confronts many children when they leave the
sheltered home environment and are thrown completely on their own as they start to school for the first time.
This is all the more acute if the child harbors any doubt
in his mind that one parent (especially the mother) may
not be there when he returns. It is also true that nail-
biting, asthmatic troubles, headaches, stomach pains,
eczema, twitchings, and bed-wetting are often, as
many psychologists agree, outward expressions of
inner isolation and loneliness.

When a small child experiences bereavement, it can
last throughout his entire life. Many studies have revealed that bereavement brought about by divorce
causes a small child to suffer more and for a longer time
than bereavement caused by death. It is assumed that
the principal reason for this is the sense of rejection involved. Most children will reason that a dying parent
(save by suicide) did not choose to die, while there is no
avoiding the fact that in divorce one parent did leave by
choice. Also most children understand enough about
the finality of death that they do not usually hold out
much hope for a reversal of the situation. However, as
long as the lost parent is still alive, there is often the
painful longing and hope that the loved one will still return and the family will become a unit again. A large
number of children feel (albeit unrealistically) responsible for the failure of the marriage, and thus their loneliness is compounded.

When the trauma of divorce is experienced by the child during the first eight years of life, the effect in causing a strong vulnerability to loneliness is often quite permanent, continuing well into his adult life. However, the older the child is at the time of the divorce, the less permanent its effect seems to be on continuing vulnerability to loneliness.

The fear of loneliness and the strength of its effect in the lives of young children can be seen in counseling brutally abused children. They often refuse to testify to the brutality of their parents and express a desire to return to them even in the face of obvious abuse. It appears that in their minds any parent is better than no parent and the fear of being left alone.

But what of the children who are not called upon to face the tragedies of death, divorce, and brutality? Are many of them also lonely? The answer is yes. A great number of them are very lonely. Several other reasons for such loneliness should be mentioned.

With such a large number of homes in which both parents are now involved in full-time jobs, it is natural that in too many of these homes too little time is left to share with the children. Not only are they lonesome for more contact with their parents, but they also often come to feel they are troublesome, excess baggage that must be shifted from home to baby-sitters, to school, back to baby-sitters, and home again.

Many parents are caught up in the "we count too" freedom of the day. While it is important that they should have some time for themselves, it should not always be at the expense of the children, and a balance should be kept in meeting the total family needs.

Another factor which often helps cause lonely feelings for young children is unreasonable expectations of parents, teachers, and other adults. They often expect more of the children than the children can deliver. This not only leaves them feeling inadequate, but the injury to their self-esteem causes them to feel that others think as little of them as they think of themselves.

Closely related to this is the fact that uptight parents or teachers are often prone to put the children down, emphasizing their faults and failures rather than their abilities and successes. This is often an attempt to deny any personal responsibility for their less than perfect behavior, but it leaves the children feeling deeply lonely and rejected.

Many children today have fewer close friends with whom to share their difficulties, as well as their joys, than children of previous generations. One reason for this is the time element in the hurried lives so many families lead. Another is the relatively small amount of time many families spend at home and the amount of time spent in the home which is given over to the media. An important reason, which should be mentioned, is the nonsocial nature of many homes and communities today which give the children little help in making friends and learning social skills.

One element which I consider of utmost importance is that children are rarely taught the joy of being alone. On the contrary, they are too often led to believe that activity and friends are necessary for happiness, and being alone is something to be avoided. When this attitude prevails, they miss much of the source of inner growth and creativity that springs from time spent alone. They tend to grow into adolescents who feel they must always have noise, people, and frenzied activity about them if they are to be happy, or even comfortable.   •

The Adolescent

The period of adolescence is the developmental period when the greatest times of loneliness seem to come. The adolescent has a great concern about "being somebody." At the same time he has a great feeling of commitment to himself. He wants to be identifiable as an individual capable of making his own choices. While overall suicide rates in the United States have remained fairly constant for the last decade, suicide rates for adolescents under twenty have almost doubled, making suicide one of the major causes of death for this age group. In some regions of America, it is second only to accidents in the cause of death.

This period of life has been referred to by some as "the halfway house" stage of life. Adolescents are neither children nor adults and often feel they do not fit in anywhere. Their rate of growth varies so greatly that many of them either find themselves lagging behind their peers or greatly advanced in physical maturation and thus feel set apart from the group. It has been suggested that the biggest reason for school dropouts may not be the lure of money or the desire for independence but a hunger for acceptance and the unrealistic hope that they may find it in another place or another role.

This feeling was expressed in a poem by a high school student who wished to remain anonymous:

Confusion

What am I? Who is he?
Who is the person whose name they gave to me?
How can I be what they expect of him
Until I know who he is?
I can answer when they call his name,

But I feel like a fake each time
For I don't really know such a person.
I have searched for him in other people's eyes;
In their voices as they called his name,
But their eyes and their voices said
   they did not really know him.
So I searched in other places.
I searched the dreams that come
   in the long night.
I searched in the dreams that
   occupy the day.
I searched the cold trembling down inside me
   that wants to find a friend.
But you can't make a friend until you're someone.
And you can't be a someone without a friend.
Cruel dilemma!
I wouldn't think a nobody could be so lonely!

An interesting observation has been made by Dr. Joseph Hartog (in *The Anatomy of Loneliness*) about the two contrasting ways youth groups deal with loneliness from diametrically opposite positions. The conformists handle it by huddling closer to their kind, attacking outsiders whether they come from the next block or from another country. The nonconformists try to deny their loneliness and need for conventional acceptance by withdrawing, in behavior and appearance, from their own family's culture. Both groups have in common the fact that they attempt to displace and project their authority conflicts, the conformists on strangers and the nonconformists on their parents' society. At the same time, they both use the conflict to establish closeness with likeminded individuals in a group. If they are unable to do this, or if the closeness they establish seems artificial to them, they are often left with a deep loneliness.

It has been over four decades since I learned the painful lesson of how lonely a teenager can be, but the hurt is still with me. Nobody liked Helen. Most of us steered clear of her. I wouldn't have known her, but she roomed with one of my best high school friends in the boarding school we attended. I got frequent reports of all of the mean, unfriendly things she did, like dumping freshly ironed clothes into the shower, or tying shoestrings together with impossible knots just when someone was in a hurry, or hiding reports the night before they were due.

She was a puzzle to me. She didn't look tough, even if she did work so hard at the image. Her large, blue eyes looked more sad than mean. I mentioned this to my friend, Marty, but she said I was wrong, dead wrong. She said I should try living with her.

Then the week before Christmas holidays my mother made lots of her best Christmas fudge. She let me wrap several small boxes of it for my friends in the dormitory. I had delivered all of them except Marty's. When I went by her room, Helen was the only one there. A look of disbelief came across her face as tears came into the big, blue eyes.

"You brought *me* a gift?" she asked incredulously. "How *could* you? Nobody ever ..." and she choked on her words.

I dared to put my arm around her as I asked, "Nobody ever what, Helen?"

"Nobody ever in my whole life liked the way I am. So I decided if nobody was going to like me, I would *make* them remember me by doing mean things."

She was crying harder now and was evidently embarrassed by her self-revelation and by our nearness. She ran into the bathroom and locked the door. I could hear her quiet sobs, but she didn't say anything for a long time. Finally she broke her silence with, "Thanks for the present but please go away!"

I left to go find Marty to tell her what had happened to her present and to swear her to secrecy.

I thought about Helen often during the holidays and wondered where she was. I knew her parents were dead and that she felt her older brother and sister did not want her around. We were not surprised when she failed to return after the holidays. She was failing all of her classes and was under a threat of suspension for her behavior.

We *were* surprised, though, and very dismayed, when the word came some months later of her death by suicide. I kept hearing her words, "Nobody ever in my whole life liked the way I am."

That's a hard conclusion for any human being to face, but especially hard for adolescents who care so much, whether they admit it or not, what others think of them.

The Young Person

When we speak of loneliness in America I suppose many Americans feel as I did that youth is a happy, carefree time when loneliness would be less prevalent. We see old age, on the other hand, as a time of sitting alone, looking sad and feeling a deep longing for the days and the people gone from their lives. However, I was quite surprised to find just the reverse to be true.

In all of the surveys I studied, and to a lesser degree in the ones I conducted myself, I found the younger people to be more lonely than the elderly.

I was also surprised to find that in the surveys I recently conducted in middle Tennessee, the college-aged young people rated themselves as significantly less lonely than those who had participated in similar surveys at New York University, the University of Denver, and at UCLA. Perhaps this can be accounted for, at least partially, by the fact that students I surveyed were in a much smaller university, in a much smaller city, than any of the other three, and thus they probably find it much easier to make friends and become known. Another related reason may be that most of these students come from a fairly small radius of the surrounding area and thus not only have similar backgrounds but are more able to keep their home ties intact while in school.

However, my surveys agreed with those from other areas in some important findings. The most dramatically evident of these was the definite relationship between a poor self-concept and loneliness. Perhaps this helps to explain why divorce and other detachment experiences during childhood produce loneliness in adulthood. Related to this is the fact that people who do not like themselves are often found not to like other people either. This would naturally make friendships harder to form and thus increase loneliness.

Another relationship which was found to be of very definite importance in all of the surveys was that between the amount of intimacy a person had experienced during childhood in his own family and loneliness in later life. In my surveys it was quite evident that in

most cases those who had felt real intimacy in their
homes while they were growing up were the same ones
who had later been able to build intimate relationships
with others outside their homes. Those who had these
relationships definitely perceived themselves as less
lonely than those without them.

Besides poor self-concepts and poor family intimacy
experiences, I found several other prominent characteristics among lonely young people. They were more
dissatisfied with their lives in general. Much of this dis-
satisfaction seemed to center around their confusion
over what to do with their lives, an impatience to find
their own niche or profession.

There also seemed to be a tendency among these
lonely young people to compare themselves to others
around them and to feel that everyone else was happier
or had more friends or more sense of purpose than they
had. Like young Bill at the beginning of this chapter,
they tended to stand at the dormitory window and,
hearing laughter, feel that only they were not laughing.

Because of their preoccupation with their unanswered questions and their feeling of isolation, these
young people tend to become self-centered in their
thinking. This feeds their feeling of loneliness, for loneliness seems to flourish best in the soil of self-centeredness.

Of course, those young people who enter college
away from home find the change is often abrupt. They
have just come through the high school stage of their
adolescence when they based a lot of their self-concept
on the praise and acceptance they received from their
peers, families, and community. Now they are sud-

denly thrown among strangers, and that validation is not always soon forthcoming.

One condition, which very often brings a keen sense of loneliness at any age but which is particularly noticeable at this time, is the disparity between idealized or hoped-for goals and the reality which one faces. Most young people have long looked forward to this time with the expectation they would find independence, love, and success. But in reality, they often find there is no magic about growing older that guarantees these things. They are as illusive as ever. Many young people, instead of realizing how many of their peers are facing the same experiences, feel they must be among the unfortunate few who are missing out on all of the hoped-for joys.

Perhaps we should not be surprised to find such a high rate of loneliness among young people. We have but to listen to their songs, their poetry, and look at their heroes to recognize their feelings of frustration, alienation, and loneliness.

The Young Adult

Loneliness in our adult population often centers around core sociological problems in our present society, the high mobility rate, the competitiveness, the dearth of meaningful relationships.

We often see the loneliness men and women feel in business, both in their offices and in their travels. The antagonism that exists in big business leaves them yearning for trust and real friendships which are almost impossible within the spirit of competition that exists. They feel they must keep themselves hidden from others for fear some weakness may be shown which will cause them to lose their place on the ladder of success.

When those persons come home to what appear to them to be a lot of trivial household problems and to seeming lack of understanding about the strain they have faced all day, they feel angry, disappointed, and lonely.

However, there are compensations built into work, such as success, challenges, and achievement, which tend to make the unhappiness and loneliness easier to live with.

The businessman's wife, on the other hand, may feel none of these compensations. She not only feels separated from her husband and his work but also from the resources of culture, community, and people which make life interesting and worthwhile. She feels left behind in knowledge, participation, stimulating growth, and influence. This leaves her feeling cut off, not only from people but from a part of her own self. This leads to an intense loneliness.

In his book, *The Pursuit of Loneliness*, Philip Slater describes the condition of the lonely housewife:

> The emotional and intellectual poverty of the housewife's role is nicely expressed in the almost universal complaint: "I get to talking baby talk with no one around all day but the children." ... The idea of imprisoning each woman alone in a small, self-contained, and architecturally isolated dwelling is a modern invention, dependent upon an advanced technology. In Moslem societies, for example, the wife may be a prisoner but she is at least not in solitary confinement. In our society the

> housewife may move freely, but since she has no-
> where to go and is not a part of anything anyway
> her prison needs no walls.[1]

The suburban housewife has often been called "the
new servant class." The family's second car has caused
her to spend two or three hours a day as an involuntary
chauffeur.

This is but one of the servant roles the suburban
housewife is expected to play. She is responsible for the
physical care and management of an ever-enlarging,
status-proving home for which she cannot find the in-
expensive help available in past times. She must spend
her time on things rather than on people.

In a study done by sociologist Alice Rossi (1972), 65
percent of the women surveyed reported that they con-
versed with their husbands less than two hours a day.[2]
The research also showed that even the full-time home-
makers spent less than two hours a day in interaction
with their children. By contrast, they devoted more
than twice as much time to household chores as to the
combined time of interaction with both their husbands
and their children.

Most of these women had entered into the arrange-
ment under the deception that they were accepting the
isolation and lack of growth involved in order to provide
better communication to their husbands and children.
Instead, they found most of their energies used up in
menial, boring, and uncreative tasks that were for-
merly assigned to maids. While it is true that a large
number of housewives are now working outside the
home (with another set of problems), still a great many

wives who started out with an idealized concept of devoting their lives to the home have found this substitution of menial, routinized tasks for interpersonal and creative endeavors has brought them a sense of loss and loneliness.

On the other hand, those wives who have found it necessary, or preferential, to work outside their homes have often found they have stepped upon a mad merry-go-round of work, child care, chauffeuring, and housework which leaves them little time for themselves or for their families. Thus they, too, feel a sense of loss and loneliness.

In either situation the unhappiness and restlessness is often accentuated by unstable marriages. A true marriage of love and trust and mutual striving could help them transcend many of these problems, but such marriages are becoming too rare in our society today. A disturbing number of couples who come for marriage counseling find that each of them has longstanding personal problems with which they must deal separately before they can begin to work on problems of life together. Just recently I heard a young teenage girl, whose life had been greatly frustrated by her parent's divorce when she was six years old, answer the question whether or not she ever expected to get married. She said, "Yes, I want to marry. But I want to wait until I am absolutely sure who I am. For how could I possibly choose the one I want to combine my life with until I know that?"

I felt she showed a wisdom beyond her years, perhaps born of the sad experience she expressed, when she said, "There was no way my two parents could have fitted their different personalities and life-styles into a happy marriage."

The Median Adult

A stage in adult life which has come to be recognized in recent years as fraught with loneliness and depression, as well as increased suicide rate, is that of the mid-years. A phrase from Dante has been used to describe this period as "the dark wood." A great number of both men and women have driven themselves fiercely during youth and young adulthood and then have come to this time when they stop and look backward and to the years ahead and realize they are never going to make all of their dreams come true, and they feel acutely alone. For the man, the disappointment and despair of this time usually centers around his career as he begins to realize he really isn't going much further. For the woman, it often centers around the empty nest, the leaving of the last child from home and the loss of her main sources of meaning and usefulness. For both, it may well involve a new, realistic, and sometimes disturbing, look at their marriage as they are no longer held together by family obligations.

The importance of this period was stressed by Carl Jung (1933) in his *Modern Man in Search of a Soul.* In treating people with difficulties of midlife, he insisted that a different approach was needed. He reminded us that we need to distinguish between "the psychology of the morning" and "the psychology of the afternoon." He insisted that all of the patients he has treated in this second half of life had lost hold on the religious concepts necessary to face the horizon which is bleak without a God because only emptiness lies ahead. He remarked that he had never been able to find real healing for any of them until they had regained their religious outlook.

The Senior Citizen

When the average person thinks of old age, he assumes it is a period of loneliness because it is a period in our world today when most people either live alone or in retirement or nursing homes, separated from old friends and family members. This idea equates loneliness with being physically alone.

However, it has been found that on this level of loneliness many of the aged fare better than younger people. They expect to be alone. They have had long periods in which to anticipate it and prepare for it. Most of their peers are in relatively the same position. Unlike the college youth referred to earlier, they are not surrounded by an active, laughing crowd that makes them feel different. Many of them actually enjoy the peace and quiet of these years and do not long for a lot of company and activity. Actually, their loneliness often comes from a need for time and for space for solitude. Aged persons who live within busy families, or at some retirement homes aimed at togetherness, often feel a need for a certain essential privacy in order to keep their integrity and individuality.

Some writers have contended that desolation—a deprivation of a love relationship—more than isolation —or having to live alone, secluded from family and friends—is the major cause of loneliness in old age. The death rate in widowhood is much higher for the same age ranges than for those who are still living with a companion. They point out that this is especially true for males.

This is not to indicate that there are not still many older people in our society who *are* lonely just from lack of friends or families or the feeling that someone really cares. The whole world was touched by a report a few years ago of the death of an elderly lady. Among the possessions she had left behind, they found a diary. On every page for the last year of her life she had written only one sentence: "No one came today."

Another news announcer told of receiving a letter from a lonely lady who said she stayed awake until the last program was over every night, refusing either medicine or sleep, because she wanted to hear a human voice say, "Goodnight to you."

As I mentioned in my book, *When All the Bridges Are Down*, some of the loneliest people I have ever met were in a psychiatric hospital, where it is easy to get the feeling that your illness has permanently separated you from everyone else. Some of the feeling of this isolation and loneliness was expressed so well by Elizabeth Tabor in *The Cliff's Edge: Songs of a Psychotic* (1951):

Panic

And is there anyone at all?
And is
There anyone at all?
I am knocking at the open door . . .
And will it open
Never now no more?
I am calling, calling to you . . .
Don't you hear?
And is there anyone

Near?
And does this empty silence have to be?
And is there no one there at all
To answer me?

I do not know the road ...
I fear to fall.
And is there anyone
At all?[3]

In Summary

As I pointed out early in this chapter, the pain of loneliness is, indeed, universal. This was expressed so powerfully by Thomas Wolfe in *The Hills Beyond*:

> Loneliness, far from being a rare and curious phenomenon ... is the central and inevitable fact of human existence. When we examine the moments, acts and statements of all kinds of people — not only the grief and ecstasy of the greatest poets, but also the huge unhappiness of the average soul, as evidenced by the innumerable strident words of abuse, hatred, contempt, mistrust and scorn that forever grate upon our ears as the manswarm passes us in the streets — we find, I think, that they are all suffering from the same thing. The final cause of their complaint is loneliness.[4]

It is truly a part of our human predicament, known to all groups, in all places, at all times. In the pages ahead I hope we can look at some of the causes of the recent increase in the problem in our nation. I hope, too, we can come to see that the problem is not without hope. Rather, much of the great human need that is reflected in the problem of loneliness can be converted into a deeper understanding of ourselves and of our common humanity.

Notes

1. Philip Slater, *The Pursuit of Loneliness* (Boston: Beacon Press, 1970), p. 68.

2. Alice S. Rossi, "Family Development in a Changing World," *American Journal of Psychiatry*, 24: 1057-1066.

3. Elizabeth Tabor, *The Cliff's Edge: Songs of a Psychotic*, quoted in Frieda Fromm-Recichman, "Loneliness," *Psychiatry* 22:1-15.

4. Thomas Wolfe, *The Hills Beyond* (New York: Harper Brothers, 1941), p. 186.

2
The Growing Nightmare

Just this week I listened to some parents of teen-agers in one of our Western states as they were inter-viewed concerning their pain and bewilderment. They felt the lives of their children were totally beyond their control. They spoke of the speed with which every-thing seems to be moving in our changing world. They felt their teenagers were ruining their lives with drugs, alcohol, free sex, and no respect at all for authority. But they felt that they, as parents, were totally helpless to do anything about it.

One mother said she felt she was just dangling out in space, and someone had cut the umbilical cord that had tied her to her child and with it the last vestige of con-trol was gone.

One parent said he did not see what any parent could do, short of chaining his children to a bedpost and never allowing them to leave the house. He said, "Once they walk through that door, we have no control over them at all. They look only to their peers for direction."

"I had thought maybe it was just the nature of the control of the peers in the town where we lived," an-other mother said, "so I moved to four different states in different parts of the country. With each move, it only got worse."

They seemed so desperate, so sad—and so familiar. All over our nation we hear people, not all parents, but young people, teachers, ministers, police, people from all walks of life, decrying the changes taking place in our nation. And they all agree that these seem to be growing at a fearful rate.

Behind many of these changes lie the causes of the increased loneliness, alienation, and despair we have been talking about.

As we look at some of these changes, I want us to look at two different kinds of change I see taking place: the changes in the circumstances in which we live, or the sociological changes, and the changes in attitudes and value systems, or the psychological changes which are evident in our land.

Perhaps the most obvious, and the one which affects the life-style of more people, is the vast increase in the mobility of our nation's population. Two television dramas, geared to family viewing, which have enjoyed long runs in recent days have reminded us all how different our lives have become in a relatively short time. "Little House on the Prairie" portrays a time when the community was small and everyone in it seemed like part of the extended family of everyone else. A trip to the nearest town in a wagon was a big event. "The Waltons" portrayed times only forty or fifty years ago, and yet if anyone new came through the little mountain community, he was recognized by everyone as a stranger. When World War II came it was the first time members of the Walton family were called upon to leave the closeness of the family circle to go to faraway places.

Most of our younger generation watch these TV

dramas from a curiosity to see "how things were back then," in a time and an atmosphere they know little about. Those of us who were young in the thirties and forties watch them with nostalgia and with a certain sadness for what we realize will never be again.

When I was a child and my father was a college professor in north Georgia, we were the envy of a lot of our friends once every year because we got to take "the long, long trip" to southern Illinois to visit our grandparents. My husband and I went back there recently, and I was amazed how short a trip it is today. As we drove back home I thought of my own five children and how different their lives have been from mine. All five of them have lived on at least two continents and have attended school with students from at least fifty other nations. They hold degrees from colleges and graduate schools in eight different states. Three of our sons with their wives were in Europe at different times one summer, and one of them traveled around the globe with his family from their former home in Morocco to their new home in Japan. More recently this son and his family came to America for three months, and another son and his wife went to Japan. Two of my grandchildren have been in a dozen or more countries on four continents.

When my husband and I moved to Nashville, it was our thirty-first move in twenty-four years of marriage. The thing about all of this which is most germane to our discussion is the fact that our life has not been all that different from many of our peers. Constant moving and a wide variety of experiences are becoming par for the course in our country today. Forty million Americans change their place of residence every year. Even when you take into consideration the remaining small town and farm families who rarely move, still the *average* American has moved fourteen times in his lifetime. Some American schools report a 50 percent pupil turnover in any school year.

Studies show that these nomadic children do not fare that much more poorly in their academic work than their less mobile peers. However, the studies show these children are participating much less in extracurricular activities, entering less into the spirit of the schools, and forming fewer close relationships. They seem to have a feeling of impermanence that leaves them feeling everything is too temporary in nature to make it wise to become very involved.

This high mobility rate has caused a great percentage of our people to no longer want to become attached to *things*. Perhaps this is a defense mechanism so they will not be hurt by the impermanence they feel. Perhaps it is just a matter of practicality. Since they know they will move often, they have learned the wisdom in "traveling light." It doesn't take many moves to cure one of having to pack a lot of possessions, pay to move them, and unpack them again. This encourages a practice already growing in our country to buy disposable things. We have been referred to as "the throwaway generation." I felt the epitome of this came when we began to see advertisements for paper bridal gowns which, like many of our present graduation robes, are disposable. Already I had seen the offer from a toymaker to let little girls trade in their dolls for newer models. When I remembered how long my only daughter held onto all thirty-eight of her dolls not twenty years ago, and how carefully through the centuries women have packed away and stored their wedding gowns for safekeeping, I realized anew how much, and how rapidly, our way of life is changing.

If we could feel that this lack of attachment to things meant a real change in our national psychology, so that we were coming to value *people* and *being* more than *things* and *having*, it would be a welcome change indeed. But I do not believe that there is much evidence that this is what is taking place. The constant change, with the feeling that everything is temporary and not worth bothering to hold onto nor to cultivate, seems to be carrying over into personal relationships also. We will discuss this dearth and its cost in personal security and satisfaction a little later. But first I would like for us to look at some of the reasons for this increased mobility.

The pressure to provide a higher life-style, which skillful advertising through the media has convinced a large number of American families is needed, keeps many of our young families ready to move anywhere, anytime there is an offer of a promotion, a possibility of going one rung higher on the ladder of the pay scale.

A restlessness, a lack of roots, perhaps a subconscious search for meaning, has given many Americans a compulsion to "keep moving on." The next house, the next town, the next job, seems to hold out a hope for meeting the not-too-clearly-defined needs behind the restlessness.

There are fewer strong ties to hold people in any one place than there were a few decades ago. The fragmentation of the family by divorce and separation and the dissolution of the extended family into retirement villages, nursing homes, distant jobs and schools, all help to destroy those ties which once held families closer together.

A smaller percentage of our people own their own

homes and thus feel it is easier to pick up and move wherever the job market, or other enticements, lead them. Fewer family dwellings are available at an affordable price. Many people do not even own much furniture. They can rent furnished apartments or can rent the furniture separately from one of the numerous rental agencies without having to worry whether or not it will fit into the next apartment in the next city. In analyzing the preferences of apartment dwellers, many urban planners have referred to the great preference for "minimum involvement housing." This refers to a desire not to be involved in upkeep, lawns, utilities, etc., but it also refers to a desire for all of the privacy possible with no expectations upon them that they are to share recreation or responsibilities with their neighbors. This places a tremendous responsibility on the family to meet all of the social, recreational, and other needs of their own family without outside aid.

Even when a family stays in one general area long enough to become more established, there is often constant moving between various apartment complexes or a constant change of neighbors within a given complex. This also discourages the forming of meaningful relationships.

Many people work in continuous operation plants and offices and work different shifts from their neighbors. The fact that they sleep while others work promotes the tendency to isolation and uninvolvement.

Another change in the circumstances in which American families find themselves is the tremendous move toward urbanization. Agriculture, which was for such a long time the basis of civilization, has lost its dominant place in country after country. In a dozen of our leading countries today, agriculture employs less than 15 percent of the working population. In the United States this number has fallen to less than 6 percent, even though we continue to feed 200 million Americans and the equivalent of over 160 million others around the world. The large cities of the world are growing at a rate of 6.5 percent a year. This means the world's urban population doubles every eleven years.

The crowded cities mean a different kind of living for most of the people who move there. A large percent of the available dwellings for newcomers to these cities are small apartments in large apartment complexes. The rush and noise of city life, the time consumed in traffic, the impersonal atmosphere in which few people know their neighbors or even chance to live close to someone with whom they work, the fears generated by high crime rates, all cause most people moving to the cities to isolate themselves in their own small quarters with little opportunity for developing friendships or a sense of community.

Another circumstance which affects all of our lives, our self-concepts, and our distrust of our neighbors is the extreme technological advance in recent years. The use of computers and other such data-processing equipment has led to an increased feeling among our citizens that they are mere numbers about whom even insignificant information is being stored up to be used against them at some later date. Many who have applied for employment or for credit have been amazed at the amount of information the computers have amassed under their numbers.

Another element of the technological society which

creates apprehension and distrust is the ever-increasing number of both private and governmental investigators who spy upon our citizens, invade our privacy, and retain all of the information gained in giant memory machines. One private investigation company in a Southern city boasts that they alone have six thousand investigators working for them in states all across our nation. Our US government admits to employing thousands of investigators, totally aside from those involved in espionage.

Most of the large department stores admit they have hidden monitors in the dressing rooms where customers try on clothes. They watch to be sure customers do not conceal merchandise on their person or in their bags. Hundreds of large apartment houses have installed monitors to check arriving guests. The monitors can be seen by any person in the building on their closed circuit TV. The original idea was to allow a person whose bell rang to switch on the TV and find out who wanted to come in. In practice, however, many apartment managers admit that a great number of their residents prefer "people watching" to the regularly scheduled programs and spend their evenings watching who has come to see whom. This means there is no such thing as privacy if you choose to call on your friend, your psychiatrist, a wig salesman, a palm reader, or anyone in such a building. In numbers of office buildings, listening devices (sophisticated versions of the Big Ear toy advertised for ten- to fourteen-year-olds for eavesdropping) pick up conversations many feet away or in adjoining rooms or at distant telephones. Monitoring devices that can pick up conversations thirty feet away have been placed within the spindles that hold rolls of toilet tissue.

At no time will a person encounter a greater invasion of his privacy than when trying to find a job, especially with the US government. The many-paged tests which often are given include many irrelevant questions about the applicant's family, including parents and siblings, spouses and children, about their beliefs, their sexual practices, and many other things the employer has no right to ask.

The most objectionable of these are a lot of indefinite questions (often verbal), the answers to which depend on the interpretation of the one giving the test but which are put down as facts in the permanent record of the applicant. For example, if a person should be so unfortunate as to blush when asked if he has ever engaged in homosexual activities, it may well be put down on his record as "questionable." Many companies resort to the use of admittedly inaccurate lie detectors in screening employee applicants. Lie-detector firms report that in earlier times nearly all of their lie detectors were sold to police departments, but that at the present about 75 percent of them are sold for the purpose of screening prospective employees.

There isn't time or space to mention more, or perhaps these examples are sufficient to remind us how dear our privacy has become. I keep remembering what Alan Barth said about respect for privacy in his book, *The Price of Liberty*, "It is in this, as much as in any other single characteristic, that the free society differs from the totalitarian state."[1]

It seems a paradox that while the people in our highly mobile society see themselves as less attached to things, every year still brings an increase in the num-

ber of items from our technological society which more
people deem necessary in the home.

Not long ago I was helping a lady on a limited income
prepare for a move into a government-subsidized apartment. I was impressed by the number of things she
considered essential—not one of which my grand-
mother had ever owned in her lifetime, and which I had
not owned in the early years of my own marriage: a tele-
phone, an air conditioner, a steam iron, an electric
stove, a phonograph, a TV, an electric skillet, a dish-
washer, a vacuum cleaner, and an electric blanket. She
referred to her possessions as "just the bare essen-
tials." She complained about the lack of an automobile
but said that three of her children lived nearby and
each had his own car, so she would get by.

The feeling that an automobile is an absolute essential is not at all unusual in our land today. Being a two-
car family was a sign of wealth not very long ago. With
the increase of teenage drivers it isn't at all unusual to
find a three-car or four-car family in middle-class neighborhoods. Creditors and others have found that in difficult circumstances the family car is the last thing most
families are willing to give up.

In a fairly extensive survey, young girls were asked
what they considered most essential in a boyfriend. A
surprising 67 percent replied an automobile. A seventeen-year-old boy in Wisconsin committed suicide
when his father grounded him because his license was
revoked for speeding. He left a note saying that without a license he would have no car, no job, no social life,
and so he had just as well put an end to his life.

After I had read of that incident I sat for a long time
trying to realize that many of the teenagers around me

would not find such desperation over the situation surprising. I kept remembering that I had dated my husband quite frequently through four years of college, and the first time we *ever* had a car to use was after graduation when his father lent us his car for our three-day honeymoon. The thing that impressed me most as I thought about it was that my experience was no more unusual for my youth than the young man's frustrations were for his. That says a lot about how quickly times change.

All of these changes of circumstances in our way of life in America have brought about a number of changes in the general attitudes of our people which contribute to loneliness and alienation, and which also make their solutions more difficult.

The first of these I wish to mention is our increased emphasis on independence in every individual. This has grown out of a belief that dependency is bad and something to avoid. What it does not take into consideration is that interdependency can be something very good and something upon which our country was founded. Travel to even a few other nations will awaken one to how much greater emphasis is put on individual independence in America than in most other places.

This begins almost at birth in America. Our babies are held less, carried less, forced to spend more time alone in their beds than the children of most other world nations. Every sign of developing independence is praised and rewarded. The sooner they can "do it themselves," whether it be tying shoes, bathing, toilet training, or whatever, the more precocious they are labeled and the prouder (and more relieved) are the parents.

Among adults, we try to minimize or circumvent any interdependence on the society in which we live. We want private homes, private yards, private transportation, private laundries, do-it-yourself skills and equipment, and self-service stores.

Coupled with this has come an emphasis on the individual rather than the community or the group. This brings with it several problems. Parents become overly ambitious for their children and encourage them in more competitiveness than they are ready to handle so soon. A few years ago when I changed from teaching third graders to teaching first graders, one of the reliefs I experienced was that these six-year-olds were not yet being pressured by competition on the ball field, and in track, bicycling, and other activities. But that is no longer true. While I can see some of the advantages of father-son participation, the ball games which I have attended have had entirely too much pressure for such young boys to handle. I've seen few angrier young fathers and few more upset children than when the umpire called an "out" contrary to the father's opinion. This spirit of competition carries over into the classroom and makes a spirit of loyalty to the group and a feeling of helpfulness hard to establish. Later, when young people are trying to decide upon careers, we often find adults trying to influence choices based on material gain and prestige rather than on contributions to be made and personal fulfillment.

There is little doubt that this competitive spirit, which is often beyond the grasp of the child involved, has a lot to do with the next prevalent attitude which is becoming a problem. This is the attitude of self-unworthiness, or a poor self-concept. Both in the loneliness surveys I conducted and in all of those I studied, this attitude turned out to be more prevalent for all age groups than I had anticipated. This characteristic proved to have a closer relationship to loneliness than any other we studied, so this is a very significant attitudinal change.

I previously discussed the effect of mobility on children in the lack of attachment to places or things, the feeling that everything is temporary, and the dearth of any lasting relationships. All of these certainly must contribute to the low self-concept. The child who does not feel that many people are important to him most certainly will feel that he is not important to many people. Nearly all adults who are old enough to remember the earlier times when children grew up in one place, near their families and family friends, will testify to the great part which the extended family and community friends played in building their self-concept.

A few mobile families are trying to compensate for this, at least in part, by becoming active in churches, community clubs, and activities wherever they move, however brief their stay may be. But the large masses of these people are not making that effort. It may well be possible that some of the lack of control the teenagers' parents feel as their children look to their peer groups is caused by the deep need for those young people to find some kind of community and interdependence which they have never previously been able to enjoy.

A related attitudinal change which has had many people worried is the tendency American people are developing toward detachment, a resolution not to get involved. Some of this, no doubt, grows out of increased fear, which we shall discuss later, but some of it is summed up in the phrase "It's just best to mind your own business."

Not too long ago I was driving home from graduate school late one night on a fairly isolated section of the interstate when I noticed smoke coming out from under my dashboard. I was alone in my little car, so I pulled over to the side of the road, got out, and lifted the hood. When I did this, the little flame that had evidently been smouldering on my engine, caught the draft of wind I let in and suddenly grew into a five-foot blaze. I had never had an engine on fire, and I was badly frightened. At first I wasn't too worried, however, for I had a local car with a university parking sticker. I was obviously an older woman alone, so I confidently began trying to stop one of the many cars passing by, many also returning from the university. I could not get a single car to stop.

I knew so little about what was happening to my car that I feared it might blow up. I reached in the back seat and got my fairly new coat and used it to smother out the blaze, but I still had a problem of how I was going to get to town, ten or twelve miles away. It happened that there had been an alumni meeting at the university that night, and a car with four of them returning to Nashville stopped, hesitantly. They saw my sticker and thought perhaps I was returning from their meeting. After checking cautiously, they decided to take me to a phone where I could contact my husband. I'm sure I should not have been so surprised at the lack of help I was able to find, for I had read of this problem across our country many times.

I suppose, though, that it has to happen to you before

you realize how it feels to be ignored in a time of trouble just because other people do not want to get involved. While I can understand some of the fears and cautions people feel at such a time, I also understand why it is becoming increasingly hard to teach children caring, responsibility, and a feeling of community.

It reminded me of an experience I had just had a few weeks before. I had the good fortune to have several exceptionally bright children in a class I had taught for two consecutive years. I had all of them well above grade level and was wondering how much further I should take them or whether I should offer some other type of enrichment activities. I had gone to several junior- and senior-high school teachers to ask their advice about what sort of thing they thought were deficiencies in the children they were getting from us. Everyone of them had given the same reply. "If they are doing that well academically don't worry about taking them further. We get a lot of good students as far as their academic training is concerned. Why don't you see if you can do anything to help give them more feeling of responsibility and helpfulness. Could you use them for peer teaching or something like that? Every year we get fewer and fewer students who can be counted on to take any responsibility. We can't count on them to man the office for a few moments, or answer the phone, or even carry messages for us, much less help at the cafeteria cash register like kids used to do."

Such an attitude is not really surprising, I suppose, if children are brought up in an atmosphere of detachment and noninvolvement. Many of them watch their parents take this same attitude in other important realms. In the realm of government, for example, great hordes of them never vote or take any active part. The "do-your-own-thing" attitude carries with it severe temptation to relegate responsibility to leaders and others, rather than to be bothered with the obligations attendant to collective commitment.

Another area of sidestepped responsibility comes with the "out-of-sight, out-of-mind" attitude which prevails in too many areas. Too many people do not care where their garbage is dumped, for example, as long as *they* don't have to see or smell it. The same attitude applies to other forms of waste.

Unfortunately, it also applies to a great many persons' attitudes toward those human beings no longer considered useful, whether they be the aged, the infirm, or the mentally incompetent. I am well aware that the changes we have discussed, such as high mobility and smaller living quarters, make it very difficult for these persons to be kept in the family as in former times. But this does not make it acceptable for a large number of our people to take no responsibility for them at all. They still deserve to have living quarters at least as acceptable as those of the rest of the family and to be remembered and loved. To do less than this is to teach our youth not only a lack of caring and responsibility but to teach them that people are only worthwhile as long as they are productive. This sets them up for feelings of loneliness and lack of self-worth in days ahead.

Another disturbing change of attitude in our nation in recent days has been the growth in a general feeling of fear. Few atmospheres are more conducive to the growth of loneliness than that of fear. One of the leading goals of a democratic society always has been to make a country safe for law-abiding citizens, but the last fifty years have seen our nation going backward in this area. Many more people today fear harm both within their own neighborhoods and from countries in other parts of the world.

Another attitude which has, perhaps, grown out of our technological advancement is the preoccupation with bigness. Some sociologists have suggested that this is a normal outgrowth of the poor self-concepts mentioned earlier. They say that the smaller our people feel themselves to be, the more they want to become a part of something big. Be that as it may, big corporations certainly seize upon this attitude in their advertising. ("Drink our soft drink if you want to be one of the in crowd!" "Do you want to be the envy of the neighborhood? Use our floor polish!") It is interesting that the advertising rarely stresses the quality or the cost but, instead, emphasizes acceptance and respect to be gained by the use of their product.

The last attitudinal change I want us to look at is one of enormous importance in dealing with loneliness. This is the attitude that having time to be alone and helping to provide that time for others is no longer very essential in our way of life. For many years such a time has been considered a key element in growth, in coming to grips with our problems, and in getting to know ourselves. In the rush of life in present-day America, the very fact that this no longer is seen as valuable is probably one of the chief contributing causes of the growth of loneliness. We will discuss in a later chapter the importance of solitude in every life.

However, I want to point out here that too many parents are taking the attitude that to be alone is bad. They try to plan enough activities to fill all of their childrens' time and act as if they are to be pitied if they do not have someone around to play with and something active to do most of their waking hours. Many parents do not even allow their children the privilege of keeping the doors to their rooms shut (as if it were an insult to the rest of the family) nor do them the courtesy of knocking before entering.

This is helping to breed a generation of teenagers whom these same parents find so objectionable because they must always have noise, company, and frenzied activity about them. As one father put it, "No wonder they have to resort to drugs and alcohol. Otherwise, how could they stand each other and all that noise that many hours of the week!"

We must, somehow, help them to learn the beauty of quietness and the joy and creative possibilities of solitude. We may not all be able to go back to the days of long hours alone at the old fishing hole, or wandering through the quiet woods on a hunt, or camping out under the stars, but we can help foster a return to the attitude that being alone can be both enjoyable and advantageous to healthy living.

Note

1. Alan Barth, *The Price of Liberty* (New York: Viking Press, 1961), p. 75.

3
The Enemy of
Personal Growth

Not long ago I was reading nursery rhymes to Paul, my two-year-old grandson, when suddenly I came to one I had been reading for half a century and saw its meaning for the first time:

> Hark! Hark!
> The dogs do bark!
> The beggars are coming to town!
> Some in rags,
> Some in tags,
> And some in velvet gowns.

"It says we are *all* beggars!" I exclaimed. "From the poorest of us to the richest of us, we all lack something we want very much."

In the same way, as I look back over the many kinds of loneliness we have mentioned in the last two chapters, I realize that none of us has escaped. We all know loneliness in some of these areas. I think the oft-quoted statement of the noted Canadian physician, Dr. William Osler, is applicable here, "It matters less what disease the patient has than what kind of patient has the disease."

How true of loneliness! Perhaps I should make it clear that I am *not* speaking of severe pathological loneliness over which no one seems to have much control. Such uncontrollable, abject misery leaves the patient without the ability to talk about it while it is in progress, and usually not even after it has passed. These people are usually totally withdrawn into themselves and their misery.

I will not attempt to draw as strict a line between loneliness and depression. Generally speaking, depression leads to inertia, a paralysis of will, a disturbance in eating habits and sexual desires, a loss of perspective, and a feeling of total unworthiness and helplessness. However, a number of these characteristics are also found in loneliness; and loneliness is often given as one of the causes of depression. Hence we must admit there is often a correlation between the two which makes it impossible to separate them completely.

As I have gone back through the many areas of loneliness we have discussed, I find that they will all fit into eight difficulties we all face at one time or another. Any one of these, if not dealt with in a positive way, can eventually destroy, strangle, choke out our confidence, our creativity, our ability to relate to others, our usefulness, and our joy in living. I would like for us to look at them one by one and at the potential harm they can bring in our lives.

Unfortunately, the way too many of us attempt to deal with loneliness is by *denial.* Many people try to escape the realization of loneliness by running away from it. They do this by plunging into intense activity that would deny such feelings by establishing a long list of peripheral relationships as if to try to disprove the possibility of loneliness. They get involved in a frenzy of activities they feel will leave no time for loneliness. They fail to recognize that loneliness and being alone are by no means the same thing. We can be desperately lonely in a huge crowd or in the midst of frantic activity. For some reason, most people fear loneliness and feel it is something to be avoided at all costs. If it cannot be avoided, then they seem to feel it is better to deny it.

This is the way I dealt with the first deep, painful loneliness I can remember. I was five years old. My preacher father had announced we were moving far away to a new location, and the church he had been serving was having a farewell dinner for our family. I could not eat. All I could think about was saying goodbye forever to so many people we had come to love so dearly. I felt I could not bear the pain, and so I slipped away from the crowd.

I hid in an old car and cried convulsive cries of anguish and sorrow for a long time. When they finally found me there, I insisted that I was quite ill with a terrible headache. I remember reaching the conclusion that no one could possibly understand my feeling, that something inside me was being torn asunder, and I was certain they would feel that such intense grief was inappropriate. I feigned physical pain because I felt that would be more acceptable.

It is unfortunate that so many adults choose this route of denial in dealing with their loneliness. In so doing, they deny themselves an essential area of self-knowledge and growth which we will discuss in the next three chapters.

A second emotion which produces loneliness in many lives is the feeling of *loss of meaning*. Sometimes this is related to the influences of being in a very technological society, as we have discussed, where many persons feel they are simply cogs in a great machine, a nameless number in a giant computer, with no chance for creativity or input into the work which claims so many hours of their lives. This loss of relatedness to a sense of personal destiny is akin to the experience of self-alienation — a longing for the true, as yet unrealized self which they feel must certainly have more meaning than they have found. There is, in each of us, an innate desire to feel unique, needed, important to someone, with a destiny which only we can fulfill. When this is denied us, there is often a feeling of living death which threatens to destroy us.

Loneliness, for many people, centers around a *poor self-concept*. As pointed out previously, in all the surveys I conducted, as well as in those from other areas I studied, there was a very close relationship between those persons who had a poor self-concept and those who considered themselves to be lonely. There was also a close relationship between this and the loss of meaning discussed above in which a person feels he is unimportant, either to his work or to his close associates in the family or community. I can certainly relate to this feeling. In my days of deep depression, recorded in my book *When All the Bridges Are Down*, I can still recall very vividly the feeling of sitting by the lake, putting my finger in the water, and watching the brief circle of ripples when I took it back out. I thought over and over of the saying I had heard when I was younger, "If you want to find out how important you are, put your finger down into some water, then pull it out, and see how big a hole you leave."

As I finally discovered, most of these poor self-concepts which bring so much misery are often self-deceptions. They are based on fallacies we have learned. Perhaps the most trouble-causing of these is the idea that our worth can be evaluated by our accomplishments. Too many of us have spent our whole lives trying to prove our worth. We keep telling ourselves that if we do things well enough, acceptably enough, if we look right, dress right, keep our houses perfectly, and always do a commendable job of the work given us to do, we will surely find acceptance. It is on this social acceptance that we pin our hopes for a sense of self-worth.

Three things are wrong with this theory: (1) the acceptance which has to be bought by performance isn't worth having; (2) since we are our own judges as to how much is good enough, we never reach the goal because we keep raising our sights higher; (3) the system works in reverse. No one wants to be friends with a perfect person. Do you like to converse with someone who knows all of the answers? Do you want to invite the best cook in town to your house for dinner? Do you want the perfect housekeeper running in and out of your house, playing friend? It might help if we could just stop and realize occasionally that we are looking for friends who accept their humanity—who sometimes cook a great meal and sometimes burn it, who sometimes have a clean house and sometimes leave it in shambles, who sometimes know the answers but oftentimes say, "I don't know, I'll look it up."

This constant striving for acceptance by accomplishments is certain to backfire eventually. Only acceptance based on *being* has enough value and permanence to be counted on. Otherwise, our self-esteem is certain to continue to fall.

With the loss of self-esteem comes a feeling of un-

worthiness. When we reach the point of *self-rejection*
we too often assume that we are being rejected by
everyone else. We often fail, at this point, to recognize
the acceptance which could be ours for the taking. Instead, we ask ourselves, "How could anyone care for me
when I am so good for nothing?"

As I will try to point out as we go along, this poor self-
concept is a contributing factor to several other negative emotions which accompany loneliness.

The fourth of these emotions I want us to discuss is
that of *a sense of loss*, of bereavement, most often of
some loved object. This loss may come through rejection, divorce, forced separation (as in moving away
from family or friends), or in death. The sense of loss
that accompanies any of these may be closely tied to the
loss of meaning discussed above. This is portrayed so
vividly in this excerpt from the poem "Lament" by Edna
St. Vincent Millay:

> Life must go on,
> And the dead be forgotten;
> Life must go on,
> Though good men die;
> Anne, eat your breakfast;
> Dan, take your medicine;
> Life must go on;
> I forget just why.[1]

C. S. Lewis describes this sense of loss so well in the
book written after the death of his wife, *A Grief Observed*:

> No one ever told me that grief felt so like fear. I
> am not afraid, but the sensation is like being afraid.
> The same fluttering in the stomach, the restless-

ness, the yawning. I keep on swallowing.[2]

He summarizes it in one succinct sentence, "Her absence is like the sky, covering everything."

This loss affects different people in varied ways. Sometimes it is felt as a loss of someone to care for, to watch over and serve, and thus to give meaning to one's own life. Sometimes it is expressed as a loss of companionship, someone with whom to share the events and feelings of the day, without whom life seems far less important and enjoyable. Sometimes it is felt as a sense of the loss of a valued presence that the one remaining keeps reaching out for on the other side of the bed or across the table.

My own father has been dead eight years, and my mother, who is eighty-seven, told me recently that she still wakes up in the night with a sense of panic. She keeps feeling over the other side of the bed trying to find someone. She says she can't get wide enough awake to decide whether it is Daddy she is looking for, or if she's afraid one of her three dead babies is supposed to be there and may have rolled off the bed in their sleep.

Grief, or bereavement, as well as the loneliness it brings, must be accepted as an inescapable part of our humanity. These feelings must be faced and dealt with and be allowed to run their normal course. The time this takes will vary for different people. It is cruel to set a time limit and expect all people to meet it.

I shall never forget the woman who came to me at one of our summer assemblies with a broken heart and a crushed spirit.

"I don't know what to do," she cried. "I can't seem to

get hold of myself like my pastor and others seem to think I should. You see, a year ago this time I had five family members who loved me and depended upon me, and now they are all gone but one, and she is dying of cancer.

"My husband died first, and then my grown, re-tarded child I had been caring for all these many years. Then one son died with cancer and another was killed in an accident. My daughter, who is the only one left, can go anytime, they say.

"I went to my pastor three weeks after the last one died. I know he is young, and it's hard for him to under-stand. But he just said, 'There's a time for living and a time for dying. There's a time for sorrow and a time for joy. You're just going to have to dry those tears and get on with the business of living.'

"Oh, Mrs. Hollaway," she sobbed, "I don't even know what the business of living is anymore. I love the Lord, and I am trying hard. Why do you suppose I can't do what's right?"

I wanted to gather her in my arms and take her home with me to Tennessee. I wanted to let her have her "time of sorrow" with no man-made deadlines.

On the other hand, I have counseled with some whose sorrow was years behind them, but who were keeping their loss alive to the extent that they could not go on with their normal lives, nor use their experience to bless others.

Like several of these experiences that accompany loneliness, it is difficult to say whether the experience of *fear* grows out of loneliness or loneliness grows out of fear. It is, at any rate, an emotion which, in our loneli-ness, immobilizes us. Fear is the fifth of these accompanying experiences I want to discuss.

In a very young child, it is often a fear of being left alone separated from the loved parent (usually the mother) from which he has not yet been completely able to differentiate himself. We often say that the young child is afraid of the dark. This can hardly be accurate because as long as he knows the loved one is near—in the bed across the room for example—there is no fear. It is doubtful this is a fear of death or nonbeing, which comes later, because he does not yet have a concept of death. It is, rather, a fear of being left completely alone with a self which does not yet have clearly established boundaries.

As he grows a little older and learns to try to please others in order to gain love and approval, the *fear of rejection* becomes a stronger emotion. Children who are abandoned by one parent during this time often grow up with a sense of rejection which they spend their whole lives trying to overcome. For example, I know a girl who was abandoned by her father during this crucial time, and she has had great difficulty in establishing adult love relationships all of her life because she is still seeking, in every relationship, the relationship she lost with her father when he deserted them.

By the time the child starts to school, the fear of failure begins to play a big part in determining attitudes and behavior. Too often this is used as a threat both by the parents and the school authorities, which just intensifies the fear which is already present.

By adolescence, the drive for acceptance by his peers brings these last two fears into an interplay between the fear of rejection and the fear of failure that controls much of the young person's life and decisions.

Once out of school, the entrance into the job market, into marriage, into parenthood, and adult responsibility brings a whole new set of fears. Most of these, however, are just new versions of the same two which have been stalking the person as they developed: the fear of failure and the fear of rejection.

The midyears of adult life bring their own kinds of fears for many adults: fear that they are "over the hill," that life has passed them by, that their dreams may never come true, and that they are not prepared for the declining years now ahead of them.

Many of those who write about the fears of the elderly speak, principally, about the fear of impending death, which many feel is, in reality, a fear of nonbeing. However, I think that one elderly lady summed up the feeling of many when she said, "I'm not afraid of dying. I'm just afraid of living until I die." They look around them and see all of the suffering, the alienation, the indignities, the utter dependence which so many of their friends are facing, and this generates a much more pressing fear than the fear of death itself.

All of these fears, so much a part of any stage of life, certainly walk hand-in-hand with loneliness. They have a tendency to immobilize us, to turn us inward, to embitter us, and to cause us to fail to utilize the optimistic, growth-producing, and useful elements in our experiences which could contribute to our lives and to the lives of those around us.

The sixth negative attitude I want us to consider probably contributes most to all the other negative attitudes we have mentioned. It is the attitude of *self-centeredness*. Without this core feeling, loneliness could scarcely exist. We will be discussing the attributes and the possibilities of solitude in the next chapter. But when a person uses solitude in self-pity and self-concern, this negative emotion grows. Perhaps it has been fostered by the competitiveness in our society and by the need to feel successful as a measure of our self-worth.

One of the most discouraging factors in our social life in America is the lack of listeners. In most groups that get together, everyone is talking or impatiently waiting his turn to break into the conversation. Very few are truly listening to what others have to say.

In his play *No Exit,* Jean Paul Sartre portrays hell as three people fastened together for all eternity. Each of them is in extreme torment because each is talking feverishly in a monologue of his own, but none of the others is listening. There is no chance for conversation or understanding or relationship because none of the three can stop his self-centered harangue long enough to hear another. It is, as Sartre evidently intended it to be, a picture of the hell on earth which many people are creating for themselves today. This attitude prevents the possibility of growth and can only lead to miserable stagnation. It is a matter of great pity that these people can rarely understand why they are so lonely.

The seventh aspect of our emotional climate in America which fosters loneliness today is the general *lack of intimacy.* Many of the sociological problems we have already discussed contribute to this. Perhaps the largest single contributory factor is the change in American homes. With the loss of the extended family, the decrease in the amount of time family members spend together and the increased divorce rate, fewer and fewer of our people are experiencing intimacy at the family level. We have already looked at the negative effect this has on intimacy at other levels later in life. Our emphasis on independence and technological advances, which make us less dependent on other people every year, has helped to bring about the situation in which millions of people can honestly say they do not have a single intimate relationship. Of course these people feel separated, alienated from the world around them. They work with others, study with others, play, have sex, even marry without really knowing each other in a deep human relationship. It is only natural that a large portion of them feel lonely. It is sad indeed to realize that these many people do not have any real opportunity to develop the truly human qualities which can develop and grow only within relationships.

The last attitude or quality of life which I want to mention is the most important of all in understanding much of the loneliness and alienation in our present world. It is the matter of *estrangement from God.*

Late in the nineteenth century Nietzsche shocked the religious world with his declaration that "God is dead." However, if we are to be honest as we look at the lives, attitudes, and behaviors of the people around us, we must surely admit that, for the majority of people in America today, God *is* dead as far as their lives are concerned. God has not abandoned mankind, but more than any other time in history, mankind has abandoned God.

At least in part, this has been brought on by the giant egotism in modern man, born of his advancement in scientific knowledge, his emphasis on independence and individuality and, perhaps, by his underlying weak self-concept which he tries to cover up by an I-don't-need-anyone attitude. He wants to be totally autonomous and self-determining. Man, in his desire to see himself as all-knowing, in complete control, sees giving these attributes to a Supreme Being as leaving him weaker and less than the powerful being he would like to be. He prefers to say that God is a fictional being invented by less powerful, less knowledgeable men than he, to fill a need within them which he no longer feels.

The greatest tragedy of this, as we shall discuss in a later chapter, is that man, in an attempt to support his theory, has come to look at himself only in the areas where he feels he fits this picture of competence, independence, and self-sufficiency. He is training himself to reject the deeper yearnings, the dissatisfactions, the unanswered questions, and the limitations he feels on a deeper level.

How little do the majority of people today realize that their estrangement from nature, from their fellowmen, and from themselves, all stems from their chosen estrangement from God. As the title of our chapter pointed out, all of this leads to a terrible loneliness which is, by its very nature, an enemy of growth.

The egotistical, agnostic attitudes just described refer to the most actively atheistic of the large masses who reject God. There is an even larger group for whom the matter of religion and faith in God never even comes up. They have been brought up in homes and in social groups where religion is never mentioned. They see in their secular lives the beginning and ending of all. Either they do not recognize the meanings of the longings and restlessness which God has put in the heart of all men to draw them to him, or they choose to reject them.

Only about half the people in America ever attend church or give any evidence of commitment to God. Even within that number who do so, too large a percentage of them are influenced by the agnostic masses and feel little real conviction in the once a week (or less often) trips they make to a church or place of worship.

To many thousands of others, their church experiences have become habits, part of their cultural heritage which they are not yet willing to deny but which are not undergirded with any great personal commitment.

The next three chapters of this book will, I fear, have little meaning for all of these masses who have no real relationship with God. Most of what I shall say about the use of solitude, ministering to the wounds of others, and creative loneliness will be based on a meaningful relationship to God through Christ.

I hasten to add, however, that if this book should chance to fall into the hands of any who do not know our Lord, it is my earnest prayer that they will not cast it aside at this point as having no relevance for them. I shall try very sincerely in the remaining chapters to show the difference a relationship with Jesus Christ can make in the problems of life such as loneliness. I shall attempt to do this not just from a theoretical standpoint but in light of vital experiences out of my own life and the lives of other fellow travelers.

Notes

1. From *COLLECTED POEMS*, Harper & Row. Copyright 1921, 1948 by Edna St. Vincent Millay, p. 103.

2. C. S. Lewis, *A Grief Observed* (New York: The Seabury Press, 1961), p. 7.

4
Solitude Versus Loneliness

Surely we have established by now the fact that loneliness is universal, an ever-present condition of our humanity. Success is a lonely thing. Pain is always lonely. To be in a place of leadership brings the loneliness of great decisions and the responsibility for those decisions. Those who have read the biographies of Abraham Lincoln are familiar with his long, solitary, silent walks as he wrestled with many extremely important decisions. Even birth itself is an experience in loneliness. Perhaps there is no time when we are more conscious of our aloneness than in the experience of death.

But loneliness is not confined to the momentous times of great events and great decisions. It can come upon you at the most unexpected times and places. It can strike in the middle of a happy time when friends are present and laughter is shared. It can suddenly overtake you in church, at a party, or at a wedding.

Obviously, it is wrong to equate loneliness with being alone. Aloneness can be a blessing, a source of growth and of joy. On the other hand, being with others does not insulate us from loneliness. It *is* true to say that loneliness is a *feeling* of aloneness, a consciousness that no one can completely share our feelings or completely understand our thoughts.

In the last chapter we looked at many of the negative attitudes which so often accompany loneliness: the loss of meaning, fear of rejection, sense of loss, self-center-edness, poor self-concept, fear of death, or nonbeing, and estrangement from God. These are all part of the painful, negative side of loneliness. But it does not always have to be so. There can be a positive side out of which can come growth and self-knowledge, a better understanding of others, and a closer relationship to God. Paul Tillich, in *The Eternal Now*, chose to differ-entiate between loneliness and solitude. He said loneli-ness expresses the *pain* of being alone and solitude expresses the *glory* of being alone.

One of the chief purposes of this book is to express the possible glory. I believe that people were given this side of their existence not just to experience pain but for learning and growth and fellowship with God. It can be a healthy, positive side if understood and dealt with. It can be a reminder of our finiteness and our human limitations. It can lead to a deeper self-awareness upon which we can build our personal integrity. It can be a source of strength and creativity.

We all have a need for solitude. I think there may be as many people suffering from the lack of solitude as there are those suffering from too much. I certainly felt this often during the sixteen years we lived in Japan. I am sure it is hard for people who have never been there to imagine the crowded conditions. If you can imagine half of the population of the United States crowded into a land area smaller than the state of California you will get an idea of the crowds. It is no wonder that more of the Japanese work at this business of developing inner solitude than do we in the United States.

The great potential in the human soul has often been manifested in those who sought creative and recreative solitude. Jesus Christ stayed in seclusion for thirty years before coming forth to spend his three years among the crowds. Even so, we are constantly reminded, as in Matthew 14:23, of his turning aside to be alone and to pray: "And when he had sent the multitudes away, he went up into a mountain apart to pray: and when the evening was come, he was there alone." This was his pattern of life. He went aside to meditate and to remember that he and the Father were One, and that he was there to do the Father's will.

How are we, then, to convert our loneliness, with all of its negative potential in our lives, into a positive solitude?

For the majority of us who have lived in the pressure and tension of lives too crowded with work, responsibilities, appointments, and decisions, this is not going to be easy. In the beginning we will surely have to set aside a time and a place where we can be certain of no interruptions and distractions. We will probably need to begin with a physical withdrawal, but, as time goes by and we learn the art of spiritual retreat from the demands of the world, we would hope to reach a time when we could withdraw into a restful, spiritual solitude at any time and in any place.

Those who have ever tried to do any counseling, or have even tried to establish a close relationship with another person, know that it is essential to be totally present to that person. You must put everything else out of your mind. You must try to remove all distractions possible, both in the room itself and such possible

interruptions as phone calls or taps on the door. Then
you must be seated comfortably with as little between
the two of you as can be arranged and then fix your
eyes and your total attention on the other person. It
takes practice.

Achieving a solitude of heart also takes practice. In
the extensive study I have recently done on loneliness,
I have come across numerous suggestions for attaining
this goal. Out of this study and out of my own experience, I want to suggest four types of encounter with
solitude which, if tried faithfully over a period of time,
should help you to reach different levels of solitude: a
oneness with nature, a better understanding of self, a
deeper communion with God, and an ability to establish
closer relationships with your fellowmen.

If you happen to be one of those rare, fortunate few
who already engage regularly in this type of experience on all four levels, I hope you realize how small a
percentage of people in America today share such a
joy. I hope you are accepting the responsibilities which
such a privilege brings and will try to help others to
enter into that joy by these or other methods.

The first step I suggest is trying to find solitude with
nature. Go to a place that is quiet, beautiful, and meaningful to you ... a mountain, a forest, the seashore, or a
quiet garden. Once you are there, rested and comfortable, allow yourself plenty of time to try to clear your
mind of all other thoughts that keep trying to claim
your attention. Then concentrate on the natural world
about you: the sky, birds, water, flowers, trees, rocks,
whatever you see. Try to commune with these elements of creation until you feel at one with the world
God made. It may take several times or several trips,

but if you begin to get the feeling of withdrawal from the rush and pressure and noise of your everyday world and begin to feel the peace of solitude, it will be well worth the effort.

I am sure that some who read this book will not be able physically to withdraw to such a place of quietness and beauty. Some may even be confined to one room. In that case, I suggest you go there in your imagination. I have tried this from a hospital bed, and it helped tremendously. Try to find a time when you can be sure of being alone, without undue interruptions, and then spend some time concentrating on a beautiful, quiet place you have enjoyed in your past ... a mountain retreat, a spot beside a lake, the seashore, a quiet garden, a serene pasture, or woods from your childhood. Try to feel you are there again. Enjoy all the parts of the scene, the smells, the breezes, the quietness, the trees, the rocks, all of it you can remember, thinking of nothing else except coming to feel at one with nature.

Once you feel you have really accomplished this first step, you may do well to go back to the same place to try the second step. This is to spend time alone with yourself, concentrating on your own inner thoughts and dreams and problems. You do not necessarily need to try to look for all of the solutions.

Just put out of your mind all of the usual interceptors, for example, "What will people think? What do others expect of me? How will I ever find time? Does this fit the self-image I am trying to project?" Just try to get in touch with your own self and find out where *you* are. What parts of your life are bringing you satisfaction and happiness? What parts are disappointing to you? What do you feel, with confidence, that you are doing right? What do you feel doubtful about? These questions do not have to be verbalized. They do not have to be these particular questions. Just be quiet enough, long enough, with your mind cleared of extraneous matter, to listen to the questions your own self wants to ask. Then think about your answers — not someone else's, but *yours.*

The next series of encounters would begin as the others have, but this time you would go to your quiet place expecting to meet God there. When you are quiet and your mind is clear, start thinking about him. Try to open your mind to him. Do not try to pray in the usual sense of the word. Just open your mind and your heart to him. It isn't necessary to try to verbalize your thoughts. He isn't going to talk to you in *words*, so don't let words get in your way. Don't hide your real feelings and your real questions behind habitual phrases. Just try opening your heart and your mind to him. He will answer by giving you new thoughts, new insights, new love for him and for others.

If you continue arranging a time and place for this kind of communion with him over a period of time, *he will let you know* when you should include another person.

When the time comes to learn to share solitude with another person, you should be ready to clear your mind of distractions, to listen, and to be totally present to the other person. You will likely begin with quiet, intimate sharing, but do not be afraid of silences. Solitude shared can be a wonderful experience. It may not happen immediately, but, if the other person desires it and tries to enter into the spirit of sharing and the mood of caring which you have set, it will come in time. If you are fortunate enough to have a friend who has been interested enough to try going through the first three steps as you have done before you work at building a deeper relationship together, you will have an even greater chance of success. However, don't be discouraged and wait too long for such a fortunate circumstance.

This use of solitude—learning to be alone with nature, alone with yourself, alone with God, and alone with another person—can help you to realize the value of solitude and how useful, pleasant, and growth producing it can be. It is a paradox that we come closer to other human beings by learning to withdraw and to be truly alone. This use of solitude can do a lot to replace loneliness with all of its negative attitudes in your life.

If you are still feeling lonely, try concentrating on the meaning of the incarnation. Remember that Jesus gave up his heavenly throne and became a man to live among us and die for our sins. He did that, praise God! But he also did more.

He became a man so that he could walk down here among us to be tempted as we are tempted, to be rejected more than any of us have ever been rejected, to bear more pain than any of us will ever be called upon to bear. Why? It was not so that God would know what we are up against down here. An omniscient God knew all of that before the foundation of the world. He bore it all so that we, finite creatures that we are, might *know* that he knew—so that never again could any person walk on the face of this earth and cry out, "Nobody understands! Nobody knows what I am going through!"

In our anguish, in our loneliness, that profound thought, that comforting knowledge, should turn our pain into a solitude that brings glorious communion as we whisper, "I am not alone! My Lord knows!"

It is a challenging thought to meditate on all that God has done with people who have been willing to meet him in lonely retreats. Elijah went to the silences of Mount Carmel. Moses spent many months in the lonely reaches of Mount Sinai. From the ancient Hebrews in oppressive captivity came some of our loveliest psalms. The black slaves in our own land, stolen from their homelands and sold into misery, produced the beautiful spirituals the whole world sings.

God waits to teach each of us so much through solitude. It is alone with him that we will become committed enough to the cause of justice to be willing to suffer for it. It is there he will help us to become convinced enough of the lost condition of the world to be ready to give our all to remedy it. He knows that we can never truly reach the center of another human being, but the more closely we become united with the center of our God, the more we can understand and love and unite with other men. He knows our lives are the battlegrounds for the forces of good and evil in this world, and, just as the angels ministered to Jesus as he fought this battle in the wilderness, God stands ready to supply the grace and strength we need. We were never meant to fight the battle alone.

"What about prayer?" I'm sure some will be asking. My answer? It depends upon your idea of prayer. If you feel as I do that prayer means communion with God, much of what we have been talking about will come under that heading. I am not referring to a one-way conversation in which we simply use God for a sounding board for our own ideas and desires. I am not talking about using God as our escape valve for all of our pent-up tensions and problems. It's fine to take them to him and "leave them there," but it is also better to give him equal time to show us what he wants done with them.

If prayer to you means being silent before God long enough to receive his directions, then we are talking about the same experience. A lot of things have been said about "the silence of God" in recent days in a fairly negative or discouraged vein. I think we need to give more attention to the possibilities in listening positively to the silence of God. Anyone who has ever spent eight uninterrupted hours with twenty-six second graders will know the feelings that prompted my poem on the subject.

God's Silence

Thank you God for making restful silence,
Loveliest of all the sounds I hear.
My ears are aching and my body tenses,
Too many sounds, too loud, too near,
Have worn me down until I realize
Even pleasant, happy sounds repel.
I catch the signal in my children's eyes:
I am no longer listening well.
I needed so to meet you here alone.
Let your silence wash my soul anew.
Listening to each silent flower and stone,
Fill my heart with joyful silence, too!

It is at the very core of our being that loneliness strikes hardest. When we can find a solitude of heart radical enough that we can hold that core, or center of our being, up to God to be united with his center, then release and guidance and comfort comes. It seems strange to us, but nevertheless it is true, that when we separate from those we love long enough to become closer to God, we often find that the withdrawal brings us closer to them than long hours spent trying to renew communion.

This is what gives meaning to the suggested exercises in solitude. To bring things into perspective, to feel our creaturehood, our relationship to the world God has made and our humanity, our oneness with all mankind, these are the things that will improve our attitude toward all. Above all, we need to feel the wonder of our spiritual nature and to be reminded that we are just operating out on the periphery of what we were meant to be.

Although I have divided the search for solitude into four steps, they can all be summed up in one: a search for the Eternal. We will find him not only in our communion with him but also in the world that he has made and in our fellow creatures as we come to see them as unique creations with specific purposes planned by him before the creation of the world. We do both him and ourselves an injustice if we fail to realize that the Source we seek lies deep within our own hearts, waiting to speak to us.

I do not suggest this path of creative solitude will be easy. There are many difficulties to be faced.

It will be looked upon by some as a selfish venture. Too many people (most of them Christians) have thought that to "deny self" means to forget self entirely or to hate one's self. That's not the way my New Testament reads. Christ assumed that, of course, we will love ourselves when he said "Love thy neighbour as thyself." When Paul told husbands to love their wives as their own bodies he added, "For no man ever yet hated his own flesh" (Eph. 5:29). We are to lose our old sinful selves so that we may gain the more abundant life, for "He who loses his life ... will find it" (Matt. 10:39, RSV).

However, too many Christians labor under the misconception that they should not even save enough time for themselves to be healthy physically or to grow spiritually. They try to serve the Lord with worn-out bodies and spiritual exhaustion which can only present to the world a distorted view of the abundant life Christ came to bring.

Christ said that "my yoke is easy, and my burden is light" (Matt. 11:30) because he was talking as one yokefellow to another who would share the load. We would be yoked with Jesus, carrying the load in his spirit and with his power. But this kind of union cannot be gained by doggedly going ahead alone to the point of exhaustion. It calls for time alone with him for renewal.

Another objection will come from the "togetherness cult." I understand completely the good intentions and helpful service of those who began all of the "prays-together, stays-together, plays-together" slogans. But they have, in many instances, been carried far beyond their original intent to the point of allowing too little time for individual solitude and growth. This emphasis on community ("Come on, Johnny, *right now!* It's time for us *all* to pray") has caused some people to feel that an expression of individual need for time alone is a denial of the rights of the group. If we can keep ourselves reminded about how much more we will have to offer the group or the family when we find time to practice real solitude, it will help us to resist the pressure of this criticism.

One objection which is sure to come in your own mind, even if not pointed out by others, is that (like most of us) you are on the busy-busy-merry-go-round in the matter of time. You just can't add on another activity, you will be telling yourself. You are probably *very* right! I was in this very mood when I wrote the following:

Sonnet to the Foolishness of It All

God, of all the forces that do battle
Within this throbbing heart and soul of mine,
It's *busyness* that threatens me the most:
Days all filled with noise and endless prattle,
Of darting here and there with scarce a sign
Your voice is speaking somewhere in the host
Of voices clamoring to make me hear,
Each calling out directions so diverse,
Insisting that my energies be put
On dissipating goals both far and near.
There's scarcely time to speak, much less converse
With you, or with my friends or neighbors, but
The thing that worries me the most of all:
As work grows bigger, meaning grows so small.

It's not one of my better sonnets, but it released a little of an emotion which attacks most of us. There has got to be a little time for refueling somewhere!

The amazing thing is how closely all of these searches for solitude are intertwined. To draw aside and get closer to the world of nature helps us feel more attuned to all creation and causes us to better understand and rejoice in our own destiny in God's great plans.

Only as we can really come to be in touch with our own humanity can we enter into the humanity of others with real caring and understanding. When we come to comprehend the likeness of all humanity, we can look at those who fail, who ache, who long for death, and say, "I could have been in those shoes." When we can face our own shame and guilt and can claim them and be willing to share them, then we can come closer to being able to share the shame and guilt with those in pain about us.

The more we come to love and trust and fellowship with our neighbors, the closer we come to our common Lord. The reverse, of course, is true. The more we commune with our Creator, the closer we come to the rest of his creatures.

A sense of meaning and purpose and joy in all of the universe, in our selves and our surroundings, our neighbors, and our Lord, will do much to deal with the negative side of loneliness discussed in chapter 3. In the pages ahead, we will look at those experiences again and see how such positive uses of our solitude should affect them.

I hesitate to end this chapter at this point for fear someone will conclude I consider this to be one of those simplistic 1-2-3-4 answers to your problems. I assure you that in this chapter I am assuming that a large number of the readers of this book will be persons who are active in the Christian life. I have already made it clear that I do not exempt you from the problems we have been discussing. We all have our times of loneliness. For many of us it is a constant problem which robs us of some of the joy and effectiveness which should be ours. It does not seem to be so serious a problem as to be interfering with the normal pursuit of our lives. But we would like to get it better under control and turn it into something positive. It was for this group that this chapter was written.

These suggestions are given with the hope that those who are willing to attempt them will find several things happening in their lives: (1) the gaining of a new sense of freedom that you are venturing out with God without too many restrictions of habitual customs and procedures but with a joyous sense of the purpose to know him better; (2) the gaining of a truer self-identity that will not be based on false or changeable standards; (3) the experiencing of a new opportunity to comprehend your own humanity and your place in his creation; (4) a feeling of relatedness to the rest of the human race that will engender new understanding and new caring.

I have already pointed out that I am not trying to deal with pathological loneliness, which is difficult, even for the experts. However, I feel that I should mention that there are many deeper problems, short of pathological ones, that we need to recognize as requiring professional help if it is available. Any one of the negative attitudes we have discussed, loss of meaning, bereavement which extends over a length of time, self-rejection, or similar feelings that persist too long or have roots too deep in past experiences, may need more help than we can give here. Suffice it to say, the majority of loneliness problems are those which are just a part of our humanity and can often be helped. Even those who need more professional help will be undergirded and encouraged by the kind of sharing and attitudes we will discuss.

We will, in the pages ahead, be considering things we can do to help others about us who are lonely. We will talk of things we can do in our own families and circle of friends to help reduce and prevent loneliness. Hopefully, we will get a new vision of both how to transcend and to use the pain of the inevitable loneliness in our lives to help others.

5
The Wound That Heals

My pastor tells a story that embodies a lot of the meaning of what I want to say in this chapter. It is the story of a very wise little girl whose mother had sent her to the neighborhood grocery to get something she needed in her baking. The mother waited and waited, but the child did not return. After a long time she saw her coming up the street, and she went to the door to meet her.

"Where have you been so long, honey? I've been waiting for you."

"I'm sorry," the little girl answered. "You see, I passed a little girl who had broken her doll and was sitting by the side of the road crying. I just had to stop and help her."

"What did you do to help her, honey?" her mother wanted to know.

"Oh, I just sat down and cried with her a while," the little girl replied.

Every time I think of that story I think to myself, "Half of the world is waiting for that kind of help!"

Sometimes the only kind of help we can give others is just to put our arms around them and share their pain. This is particularly true of loneliness. We cannot take away the loneliness of another. But we can offer our-

selves to them in love and understanding with the hope
it will help them to recognize one important key to their
suffering: *no one* is going to be able to take away their
loneliness. Too many people move from friend to friend,
from lover to lover, from husband to husband, looking
for someone to take away their loneliness. Too many
marriages are given up because one or both of the
partners is disappointed in not having found someone
to meet this need. By sitting and sharing their pain, we
may be able to help them realize that it is a common
pain which we all share because we are human, and
which we must all own and seek purpose and meaning
in for ourselves.

I do not think I would be alive today if God, in his
grace, had not sent to the midst of my despair a man
who had, himself, walked through the depths of such
misery. He had come to grips with pain and anguish
enough that he could put his own pain aside and hum-
bly come and sit and share my pain. I told the story in
the book *When All the Bridges Are Down* of how Dr.
Bill Penrod literally saved my life.

But over the last nine years I have come to know the
personal cost to him in the years of agony that prepared
him for the kinds of encounters which turned my life
around. When we are in the midst of such misery we
sense immediately the presence of a person who truly
understands and shares our pain because he has been
there. On the other hand, we are repulsed and made
worse by someone who comes and stands out on the
periphery, mumbling platitudes which say to us that
this person has no idea where we are at the moment.

I was talking with Bill this morning about some of
the price he had to pay in pain, frustration, and self-

doubt over the period of several decades before he really began to get hold of how God planned to use his experience in his ministry to others.

When he was five years old, he had to have a serious stomach operation which kept him in the hospital, alone, for several weeks. I'm sure his folks were trying to be kind and put off the knowledge of the coming pain as long as possible. Or perhaps they didn't realize how much a five-year-old can understand. But he was asked, on a Sunday afternoon, if he would like to go for a drive. He went, with great enthusiasm, only to find himself being taken to a hospital, where he was admitted with little explanation of what was to happen to him or why. The feeling of betrayal and stark abandonment remained with him for years.

This was the beginning of a series of happenings in his life which left him feeling extremely vulnerable, sensitive, and with a growing conviction that there were very few things in this life which you could count on turning out as you expect or hope.

He was physically weak from the stomach disorder in his early years of school. But repeated experiences of having what he said ignored gave him a greater handicap: that of feeling he could not communicate well with people. As this conviction grew, it took the form of a speech dysfunction which further complicated the problem.

Perhaps it was a combination of these feelings that caused him to develop a strong anxiety about being humiliated. He says he was highly motivated to do his very best, but his poor self-image and his fear of humiliation usually caused him to do an overkill on his assignments. He would prepare more than he could deliver, either verbally or written, and would end up humiliating himself after all.

This gradually developed into such a state of anxiety that by graduate school he was on the verge of suicide. This was intensified by the fact that he felt God had called him to a life of serving others, with whom he had no confidence he could even communicate. He felt called to preach the gospel with a speech dysfunction so severe that it looked impossible. He had reached the place where he did not trust his own perceptions. He said he literally hit rock bottom before he had to go to the Lord and try to find the strength and the vision to start over again.

How marvelously God has used the pain of those years to prepare him to heal the wounds of others. His own long years of feeling that no one understood him have made him unusually perceptive and sensitive to the needs of those who come to him for help. He tries to make sure that he fully understands the needs of each of them.

This same fear of not being understood has caused him, as a university professor, to study his subject matter so thoroughly that it becomes simple for him. Because of this, he is able to make even the more difficult subjects of psychotherapy and statistics seem quite understandable to his classes.

His own insecurities of the past have made him unusually sensitive to the need of others for validation. His idealism and ambition that caused him to overshoot the mark help him to realize that many others have difficulty recognizing their own limitations. He has helped a large number of us to accept our finiteness and give up some of our perfectionism and tendency to play God.

At the same time, he has kept us all reminded that when we hit rock bottom the only thing we can count on, ultimately, is the grace of God. While keeping us mindful of our finiteness, he also keeps us reminded of our grasp on infinity in the eternal love of God.

If you ask him, he will tell you that he does not resent those years of suffering, or other suffering that has come since, because he is keenly aware that he serves a suffering Savior. I think that it is very fitting that the hymn chosen for the theme of his ordination to the ministry was "Man of Sorrows."

Even one experience of receiving such help and a realization of the cost to the giver can change for life our whole concept of suffering. The pain of suffering is multiplied many times when we can see no meaning in it. Perhaps that is why we hear that common cry from those who suffer around the world: "Why? Why?"

But once you have experienced how God can use another's suffering to minister to those in pain and despair, from that moment on, the form of your cry changes. In times of suffering it becomes "What? What? What do you want to teach me? What do you want me to do with this suffering? Show me whom I can help!"

I finally began to understand what was meant in 2 Corintians 1:3b-4, "God of all comfort; Who comforteth us in all our tribulation that we may be able to comfort them which are in any trouble, by the comfort wherewith we ourselves are comforted of God."

As I think over the many trials of my life I can begin

to realize something of what God has been trying to teach me. It gives me a real sense of purpose and obligation that these experiences should be used to help others.

Our sixteen years on the mission field taught me a lot about loneliness which foreign missionaries have known down through the years. There's the loneliness of driving away from your parent's home for the last time without either of you voicing the concern you all feel about whether they will both be there when you come home on furlough in five years. There's the even deeper loneliness, years later, as the roles are reversed, and you stand waving to your own child and grandchildren as they go to serve the Lord on foreign soil. Then there's the loneliness of standing on a foreign shore and watching a ship disappear into the sunset as it carries your sixteen- and seventeen-year-old sons away to the States to school, never to live in your house again. There's the loneliness of a phone call in the night that tells you of the death of a parent ten thousand miles away, and you know that you can't be there to share the grief with your family.

You live with a sense of loneliness in a land where you are forever an outsider, a curiosity, a misfit. But your sense of isolation is never greater than when one of your group dies, and there is no funeral home, no undertaker. By law you have twenty-four hours to have the body buried, or someone will come and pick it up for cremation. The missionary men must make the wooden casket. The women must line it and prepare the body for burial. And when it is all done, you still have the problem of finding a place to bury it. For example, in Japan most of the cemeteries are owned by the Budd-

hists. Christians are not allowed to be buried there.
Only a very few cemeteries scattered across the nation
will allow you to bury your Christian dead. Death is
always a lonely time. Each of us must meet it head-on
and make our own adjustments, but it is especially lonely in a strange land.

But the deepest sorrow I learned by living in a land
where only one-half of one percent of the people knew
our Lord, was what it meant to sorrow as those "who
have no hope" (1 Thess. 4:13). We stood with neighbors
and church members and friends as they buried their
dead who had not yet met the Lord. The depth and intensity of their sorrow was far beyond that which we
know, we who have the confidence that our dead loved
ones are with the Father. I feel I gained a new confidence, a new consolation, to share with others who do
not sorrow as those "who have no hope."

Some of the deep loneliness I felt could come to anyone, anywhere, if she is in a new situation separated
from family and old friends and dependent only on her
mate or their small children for sharing. In my case, it
was a series of miscarriages. I had always wanted a
large family. When I was growing up, my friends
would tease me and say they could always read my
moods by asking me how many children I wanted. If I
was really down, I only wanted seven. If I was my normal, happy self, I always wanted a dozen! I had always
felt that healthy, intelligent women who loved children
could make no greater contribution to the world. With
all of our children more intelligent, more talented, and
better looking than we, my husband and I have never
had a reason to change our minds!

But we had our first two sons early in our marriage,

and then Ernest had to go overseas with the army. When he returned, we both had to graduate from the seminary, go up for appointment as missionaries, and move overseas. When all of that was behind us, we could hardly wait for more children. I had had so very little trouble with my first two pregnancies that I suppose I did not realize enough the need for precaution during this time. I took a twenty-four-hour trip, which we considered essential at the time, in an old, rough, early postwar Japanese train when I was three-and-a-half months pregnant. In the middle of the night, on the top bunk of a scarcely padded, triple decker sleeper, among total strangers, I lost the baby.

That first miscarriage was not only a great disappointment and grief, but by nature of the long trip I was on, the problems involved went unattended for too long a time. This was thought to be the cause of what they labeled a series of habitual abortions. I had two more miscarriages before we were able to have a live child. Eventually, I had six three-month miscarriages.

To a man, this is disappointing. But usually it is not the bereavement it is to his wife. He is excited that his wife is pregnant, but at three months he hasn't usually really identified with the child who is growing within her. So, for him, the termination of the pregnancy is just that: a disappointing termination. But for a woman, it is quite different, especially if she has found out about the pregnancy very early. From the day she is certain she is pregnant, it becomes a child growing within her. She talks to it, thinks about it constantly, makes plans for it, tries out a thousand names on it! She is very conscious of how early in a pregnancy the doctor can find a separate heartbeat, and how soon all the tiny organs form. So, when the child is lost, it is, for her, a real bereavement. One of the loneliest times she will ever know is in the realization not only that her child is gone, but that no one around her seems to realize the depth of her bereavement.

Although I eventually had five healthy children, even yet a quarter of a century later, I sometimes feel that pain. On the rare occasions when we all come together, it never fails to cross my mind what it would have been like if the other little ones I loved could have joined us. I realize that many people will consider this strange. But it has given me a real understanding of the terrible grief of women who lose children in childbirth or soon after. Knowing how attached I could become to one in three months, I can only imagine having to lose one you had carried full term with all of the long days and nights of sharing your body, your life, and your dreams.

I could go on to the death of my father or to the stark loneliness of being on the floor of the isolation ward of a psychiatric hospital with all control, all contacts, taken away from me. But that is enough of my own experiences of loneliness. I only want to add that it is my constant prayer that God will help me to use them to heal the wounds of others.

I heard someone say once, and I think it is true, that you must be willing to go *in* to loneliness and pain before you can hope to be able to bring another *out*. If only all of us who have known the pain of loneliness (and who of us has not?) could accept the challenge of the responsibility and opportunity that experience brings to give meaning to our own pain by using it to heal another's wounds.

I think nothing touches my heart more than the thought of someone suffering totally alone with the consciousness that no one around has the faintest idea of what that person is going through. A case in point is this poem which was found in the locker of a geriatric ward patient in the Greenwich District Hospital in London. The staff had not thought she was capable of writing, much less of expressing such thoughts as these. The poem is nameless and the writer anonymous, but here is the way it appeared in the hospital newsletter in *Guy's Hospital Gazette:*

> What do you see, nurses, what do you see?
> Are you thinking when you are looking at me —
> A crabbit [sic] old woman, not very wise,
> Uncertain of habit with far away eyes.
> Who dribbles her food and makes no reply,
> When you say in a loud voice, "I do wish
>   you'd try."
> I'll tell you who I am as I sit here so still,
> As I rise at your bidding, as I eat at your will.
> I'm a smart child of ten with a father and mother,
> Brother and sisters who love one another;
> A bride soon at twenty my heart gives a leap
> Remembering the vows that I promised to keep;
> At twenty-five now I have young of my own
> Who need me to build a secure happy home;
> At fifty once more babies play round my knee
> Again we know children, my loved one and me;
> Dark days are upon me, my husband is dead
> I look to the future I shutter [sic] with dread.
> My young are all busy rearing young of their own.

And I think of the years and the love that
   I've known.
I'm an old woman now and Nature is cruel
'Tis her jest to make old age look like a fool.
The body it crumbles, grace and vigor depart.
There is now a stone where I once had a heart.
But inside this old carcass a young girl still dwells
And now and again my battered heart swells,
I remember the joys, I remember the pain,
And I'm loving and living all over again.
And I think of the years all too few — gone too fast
And accept the stark fact that nothing will last.
So open your eyes, nurses, open and see,
Not a crabbit [sic] old woman, look closer — see me![1]

I have read that poem over and over during a span of
several days, and I intend to keep it handy for some
time to come, to keep reading it. I want to be sure I have
absorbed all the thoughts and emotions it brings to me
so that I will not forget their impact. How I wish I could
become sensitive enough to the other human beings
who cross my path that I would never treat them less
than that: living, caring, hurting, questioning, contributing human beings.

As I see my fellow human beings committing all the
mistakes, the wrongs, the stupid, cruel, aggressive
things, I need to remember that I have those potentials
in my own very human nature. Thank God, the reverse
also is true. All of the kind, humanitarian, sacrificial,
loving, inspiring things I admire so much in others also
have their seeds within me. We are all finite creations of
God with the potential he has placed in us for becoming
infinite. The more we realize the significance of the

humanity we share with all men, the better we can
understand our place and our responsibility in the
world.

As I tried to point out in the last chapter, one of the
most important reasons for learning to use our solitude
well is to be able to understand ourselves more completely. For in understanding ourselves we will better
understand all human beings. And until we understand
them, we cannot truly care for them. And without
caring for them, we cannot truly serve them, for service without caring is degrading.

I have mentioned, too, that so much of loneliness
grows out of self-centeredness—a looking inward with
self-pity for the loss of relationships that are gone. How
much better it would be if we could look outward toward the hundreds of people, which any one of us encounters, who desperately need such a relationship and
could fill the void within us while meeting their own
deep need.

At our house we have reached that "empty-nest"
stage of life. Because our five children were born over a
span of fourteen years, we were able to put this off
longer than some. But it does inevitably arrive. Furthermore, we are both coming nearer and nearer to that
retirement time when not only some doors of service
close within our own home but many of those in our
professions also will be closing. I was thinking about
this recently and kept remembering a phrase which
described life as the "quiet closing, one by one, of
doors." I'll have to admit experiencing a certain feeling
of melancholy until the following thoughts came to me.

Doors

One by one I watch them leave me
All the loved ones I have treasured,
Some go by death and some must walk away,
Walking now to other lives, and to other callings,
And I am left to listen to the closing of the doors.
Sometimes I feel that life is nothing
   but a long, long hallway
Filled with doors, many doors,
Closing one by one.
"But what am I to do, then,
When I hear the last door closing?"
The agony within me cries out for an answer,
And somewhere deep within my soul
I hear the answer come.
"Only *you* can close that last door,
For you control the latchstring.
The last door is the doorway of your heart."
And then it bursts upon me, like someone singing,
   singing.
It floods my long, dark corridor with light
   and vital meaning.
Each closing door has taught me something I can
   give them,
Something of love and grief and grace and
   tenderness.
Something I can share with others
As they hear their closing doors.
God has blessed me with the choosing:
I can close them out and sit here

All drying up and withering in my sorrow,
Or I can open wide the last door,
And share with them the glory
Of the meaning, precious meaning,
Of all the closing doors.
Oh, God, Thank God! Please help me.
We will open wide that door!

I am sure most of us lose sight, from time to time, of the difference it may make in the life of someone about us, and the loneliness they feel if we can but make an effort to keep open that last door, the doorway of our heart.

I remember reading an incident in Rudyard Kipling's book, *Something of Myself,* which illustrates how such opportunities to help often slip up on us unaware. He said that he and his wife, toward the end of the last century, had settled in a house in a very lonely part of New England. They could see far across a lonely valley with very few inhabitants.

One day he and his wife decided to take a walk across the valley. On the other side of the valley they met a weary old woman who asked them, "Be you the new lights across the valley yonder? You don't know what a comfort they've been to me this winter."

Then with a look of concern, she asked, "You ain't ever going to shroud them up, be ye?"

Kipling said that as long as they lived there they thought of their lonely neighbor every time they lit their lights.

The tenderness and kinship with all humanity can grow out of our own pain and remind us to never "shroud the lights" that might bring comfort to another.

I want to emphasize once more that to meet the spiritual needs of our generation we must first understand their inner confusion. This can come about by being honest enough in our solitude to admit our own needs. When we come to the point of truly feeling great spiritual need and longing, we should rejoice. This is *always* the work of the Holy Spirit. We can be sure that God is already moving to meet those needs by making us conscious of them through the work of his Spirit.

As we find time to be alone with God, we give him the opportunity to meet our inner needs. As we are conscious of his doing this, we become more aware of God's desire to meet the needs of those about us. He is constantly preparing us to help meet those needs.

We do not have to feel helpless in the face of their needs. God has not asked us to do it alone. He has made it very clear in his Word that he will perform his will in us. He asks us only to be willing to be channels of his love and grace. The promises he gave to us, he meant for all mankind. And he *did* promise, "I will not leave you comfortless." He did not say that he would send the Holy Spirit to us occasionally, or in times of great needs, or even most of the time. He promised he would send him to live within us, to be *always* there to comfort and to guide us. He promised, too, that the Spirit would teach us about him, our Savior. John 15:26 reminds us, "He shall testify of me."

Loneliness has often been referred to as "an empty space or a vacuum" within us. If we do not allow it to be filled with Christ himself and with others he has chosen us to minister to, it is nearly always filled with self, which prepares the way for even deeper loneliness. If we can, however, bring ourselves and others to allow God to fill that void, we will come to understand the true meaning of Moffatt's translation of the passage in Psalm 68 when he refers to "the God who brings the lonely home."

When God fills the void within us, he will teach us how to use each wound, each heartache that comes into our lives, for the understanding and the healing of others.

Note

1. Quoted in *The Anatomy of Loneliness,* ed. Joseph Hartog, et al (New York: International Universities Press, 1980), p. 303.

6
Creative Loneliness

One of the biggest determiners of what we make of our lives in the matter of finding happiness, peace, and the ability to make a contribution to our world, lies in the way we use our inner isolation.

Many writers on loneliness have pointed out how essential solitude is to creativity. Most works of great originality are conceived in solitude. It is, they remind us, only creative people who are not afraid of constructive solitude who will truly free the creativity within themselves. Debussy had to learn a disciplined aloneness before his creativity was loosed. When Cezanne was fifty years old he was still trading paintings for groceries. He never became a rich man, but he spent enough time alone that he saw something others did not see in the world around him and was able to translate enough of it onto canvas to gain immortality as an artist. We cannot begin to name all of those whose solitariness has brought great rewards to all humanity. Among them are Madam Curie, Gandhi, Tolstoy, Schweitzer, and Kagawa.

But solitude doesn't automatically evoke such blessings. Many times cruel and evil thoughts are produced. A large amount of the crimes of the world, and nearly all of the suicides are conceived in solitude. Twice in our era the nations of the world have been brought to the very brink of destruction by the deep loneliness and gathering isolation of a few men.

It is not a matter of whether or not we choose loneliness, but rather what we do with our loneliness. None of us can escape it. We will all have times of feeling completely alone. Even those who run from it in frenzied activity will find it in the midst of their crowds. Those who deny it will find it stalking their pathways before the sounds of their denials have faded away. We *are* human, and thus we will know loneliness.

The British philosopher, Alfred North Whitehead, in his book, *Religion in the Making*, said, "Religion is what an individual does with his own solitariness."

Augustine felt that man's orientation toward God was a part of his innate makeup when he said, "Thou hast made us for Thyself, O Lord, and our hearts are restless until they rest in Thee."

If, then, it is up to us whether we shall know loneliness with all the negative aspects we have discussed, or we shall make of it something creative and productive, what do we mean by creative loneliness? I want to mention, in the beginning, several uses we can learn to make of our aloneness which will benefit both us and others:

1. We need to spend time in quiet contemplation of our blessings, of the wonder of nature, of the majesty and order of the universe, and of the God who created it all.

2. We need to allow time for inner restoration, to clear our minds and hearts of the clutter. When we do not do this, sometimes God does it for us by putting us aside, temporarily, in a sickbed or some other form of

seclusion that he may restore our souls. I am a little ashamed to admit that there is some truth in a statement my mother sometimes makes about me. She says, "Your favorite Scripture ought to be, 'He maketh me to lie down,' because it is only when he puts you in a sickbed that you stop long enough to let your soul catch up with your body."

3. We need to use our solitude to improve our sense of perspective. In the rush and noise of the crowds, our view tends to get out of perspective and we find ourselves making decisions on false premises as the world does — success, popularity, and convenience.

4. We need to remember that in quietness is our confidence. If we abide in him we will find it much easier to obey him. Feeling at one with God and his universe helps us to regain our confidence.

5. We can, in solitude, come in direct contact with the inner raw material of our own selfhood, which is our greatest treasure.

Essential to the accomplishment of all of these, and perhaps a product of them, should be a renewed understanding and emphasis on the eternal in our lives.

Those who see only the temporal in the now of their existence must worry about the past, and more especially about the future, for there is a cutoff date "when time shall be no more." But those who recognize the *eternal now* are not bothered. They are standing on eternal ground through their faith in the eternal God. This eternal ground is not an extension of time, but is above time, above all such man-made ideas. It is based in the God who did not say, "I *know* the Alpha and the Omega," nor "I *was there* at the Alpha and the Omega," but he said, "I *am* the Alpha and the Omega,

... the beginning and the end" (Rev. 22:13, RSV, author's italics).

This puts a whole new perspective on the meaning of life. Viktor Frankl in his book *Man's Search for Meaning* says that after he had lost everything on which men traditionally fasten meaning—his work, his manuscript, his home, his wife, his freedom—he came to realize that meaning cannot depend on these perishables. He finally came to see a broader, truer definition of meaning as he wrote that if life has meaning, it must be unconditional meaning which neither suffering nor dying can detract from.

Robert Browning expressed it in another way almost a century earlier when he referred to God as the Potter in his poem "Rabbi Ben Ezra":

> Earth changes, but thy soul and God stand sure:
> What entered into thee,
> That was, is, and shall be:

Time's wheel runs back or stops: Potter and clay endure. At another point in the same poem he reminds us:

> All I could never be,
> All, men ignored in me,
> This, I was worth to God, whose wheel the pitcher
>   shaped.

We need to realize that it is in the finiteness, the temporariness of our humanity, that loneliness comes. Promises *are* broken, relationships *do* end, we are misunderstood, and we misunderstand.

We do ourselves and others an injustice when we try to evaluate relationships or time or meanings in the light of the finite. It is only in the light of the eternal that things come properly into focus. Our solitude offers us the opportunity to grasp our infinite nature, the eternal in us. We watch Christ, the God-man, constantly going aside to lay hold of this, the infinite within himself.

We need to ever keep in mind all that it means to have an eternal God dwelling within us. He said, "Before Abraham was, I am." He does not say, "I was," but always and forever, "I am." This puts a different perspective on what makes me a success, and what makes life worth living. There is a danger in putting too much emphasis on the praise, the rejection, the opinions of others. This poses a treacherous trap. Each success must top the last one. Too many successful people fall into this trap and find it destructive, a downward road to future failures and discouragements. They build up a self-image they cannot live up to and then live in fear someone will discover them as frauds.

When our emphasis is on eternal values, we can accept the task God gives us for every day without reference to the past or future or the opinions of others. It is for the *eternal now*, this little section of eternity, that we are responsible to him today.

Because I am very anxious that this approach to dealing with loneliness and solitude in our lives be practical rather than theoretical, I would like for us to go back to the six negative attitudes which we discussed both as accompanying and causing loneliness and look at them once more in the light of what faith in an eternal God should offer us in helping us to overcome them.

The first negative attitude we discussed was that of denial. We spoke of the frantic rushing of so many people from one activity to another, one crowd of people to another, one drug to another, one marriage to another, in an effort to avoid facing themselves and their loneliness. They are forever trying to find in someone or something that which they can find only within their own selves. We need to help them accept the fact that solitude is not something to be feared or run away from, but a potential good that can bring peace, strength, self-knowledge, and a nearness to God and others.

We need to remember that the element which probably frightens them away the most is that of self-knowledge. Too many are afraid that what they will find out will not fit the self-image they have tried to project. They are not secure enough in their own self-concept to be willing to face themselves honestly. This means that this problem is very definitely tied to the second negative attitude we discussed: a poor self-concept.

I can certainly understand the problem of a nebulous, insecure self-concept on the part of those who do not know the Lord. They must base their ideas of themselves on such unpredictable, transient things as the opinions of those about them as they try to read it in their eyes or in their faces, and on the amount of success they achieve on the doubtful scale by which most men measure success.

However, these things should not bother the child of God. He has no reason to have such a flimsy base for his self-worth. I am well aware that many of us do not always live this way. It took me many years to realize that a poor self-concept is an act of unfaith. I had such a low image of myself that the threat of suicide was a constant problem for me. Finally God showed me that for me, at least, suicide would be the ultimate profanity. I could not resort to suicide without saying, in effect,

"God, you sure made a mess of creating me. You made me a round person to fit in a square hole. You gave me an impossible task to do and then walked off and left me all alone with it!"

Could anything be more contrary to the teachings of his Word? My Bible tells me that God thought about me from the foundation of the world. He created me just the way he wanted me to fit into the place he had planned for me. He made me to fit the task which he had for me alone to fulfill. He placed me here in his perfect timing and promised never to leave me nor forsake me but to accomplish in me, through his strength and power, the work he has planned.

If I believe all of that, I must believe I am what I ought to be, where I ought to be, and am abundantly able to accomplish my work "through Christ which strengtheneth me" (Phil. 4:13). That doesn't leave much room for a poor self-concept, does it?

If we can slow down, stop running from ourselves long enough to give God a chance to remind us of all the things we should be able to transcend that cause many people's poor self-concept, it should simplify the problem for us.

Another of those negative attitudes which accompanies loneliness which we should be able to transcend is the fear of death, or of nonbeing. People who are not grounded in a faith in an eternal God find this difficult. Since they see their death as the end, a time when they shall cease to be, they have trouble accepting that things will go on without them. Just recently a therapist reported to me that a young woman had said that she wanted to live to be two hundred years old. She said she knew a lot of important things were going to happen, and it made her feel small and insignificant to think that the world was going to go on without her knowledge.

I have stressed the importance of accepting our finiteness and not trying to play God. I hope I have also made it clear that it is important that we realize we are made in the image of God with the potential of infinity in us.

When we accept Christ as our Savior, my Bible tells me we die with him to the old life of sin and death and are born into a new spiritual life which is *everlasting*. From that moment we have accepted our eternal ground of being. No matter what happens to our finite bodies, we exist in the mind of an eternal God.

How can we fear death if we have already died with Christ? I like the story of a Lutheran bishop in a Nazi concentration camp which illustrates this faith beautifully. An SS officer was beating the bishop severely in an attempt to force a confession from him. He wasn't accomplishing his purpose, so he kept beating the bishop harder. He finally became afraid he was going to kill the bishop before he got the desired confession from him, so he said in desperation, "Don't you know that I can kill you?"

The bishop looked him right in the eyes and replied, "Yes, I know. But I have already died."

It was as if the Nazi officer were frozen in his tracks. He could not continue the beating. What would have been the point? The beating was based on the premise that a man will give anything for his life. To one whose life already is eternal, such threats have no great meaning.

If we are firmly grounded in the eternal, we should

be able to transcend the sense of loss which increases the loneliness of so many people. Not only are our very lives rooted in the eternal, but all of those things which we treasure most are eternal. The Bible tells us that faith, hope, and love *abide forever.* The things of this world will pass away. We are not to put our hearts on the finite things about us where "moth and rust doth corrupt, and where thieves break through and steal" (Matt. 6:19-20).

We are warned, too, that prophecies will fail, tongues will cease, and knowledge will vanish away. But for his children, things can only get better. Our partial knowledge will become complete knowledge, we shall see clearly those things which are now hazy to us, and we shall come to know God as he knows us. How can we worry about future losses if we claim promises like those?

As I have pointed out, one of the very essential needs of human beings, which spawns a lot of loneliness if it is not met, is the need for intimacy. I knew God, had faith in him, tried to give my life to him in service. Still, for many years I did not enjoy the intimacy with him which he meant me to have. He was high and holy, all-seeing, all-knowing, but somehow I had not been able to claim the wonderful relationship the Bible told me was waiting for his children. What a difference it made when I finally was able to accept his constant, caring presence as a Good Shepherd who wanted to gather me in his arms and carry me in his bosom.

He has promised that no one can pluck me out of his hand. He says he knows my name and even the number of hairs on my head. For me to know him is a wonderful thought, but an even more wonderful one to me is the

thought that *he knows me!* He loves me, watches over
me, waits to guide me, lifts me up when I stumble, feeds
me, clothes me, heals me. How can I worry about a lack
of intimacy if I have available to me the only completely reliable and perfect love in the universe? One of
the miracles of it all is that the closer my relationship to
him grows, the easier it is to know and love and form
relationships with those around me.

Another of the negative attitudes which we discussed as causing so much loneliness and misery is the
fear of failure. We referred to this, somewhat, in our discussion of the self-concept. If we can truly accept the
fact that we were created by God as unique beings with
a task only we were meant to accomplish, it should remove much of our fear of failure. This is especially so if
we can remember that God promised he would not give
us any task which he would not personally accomplish
within us.

This means that any demand on our lives is a demand
on his Spirit dwelling within us. We should find comfort and confidence in the fact that our Bible tells us
that it is in our weakness that he becomes strong. We do
not *have* to succeed. We just have to allow him to succeed in us! Our sense of failure often is based on our
human concepts of time. We want to succeed right
now. Tomorrow will not do. If we can but come to trust
his eternal purposes it will relieve a lot of this pressure
we bring upon ourselves.

Another negative attitude associated with loneliness,
you will remember, is self-centeredness. If this is a
basic problem for you as a Christian, you need to exam-
ine your commitment. It is hard to imagine many
things that are so opposite to the Christian concept as
self-centeredness. Christ made it very clear that any-

one who wanted to follow him would have to deny self. We discussed previously that this does not mean hating self. We are to love ourselves enough to do the best thing we can possibly do for ourselves: turn our backs on our old finite, carnal selves, and accept abundant and eternal life through him. We are never to forget we are not our own but are bought with such a heavy price. That knowledge leaves little room for self-centeredness. However, until we get rid of our old, finite, worldly bodies, self-centeredness may continue to present a problem for us. As beings of this world we are and always will be, selfish. But the more completely we are able to give ourselves to him, the more we should be able to transcend this difficulty and be freed of the loneliness it brings.

The last negative attitude we discussed as causing or accompanying loneliness was the sense of estrangement from God. I have never forgotten my experience during my struggle with depression when I felt God had moved away from me. I had prayed with Bill Penrod and felt God so very near. Then before the weekend was over, I had a very bad time and felt like I just couldn't make contact. When I saw Bill the next time I asked him, almost in anger, "Where were you and God when I needed you so much?"

I remember that Bill replied calmly, "We were right where you left us. We didn't move. If you were away from us, you must have moved."

As time has gone by and my relationship to God has become closer, I have learned that I can count on that. If ever there is an estrangement from God it is on my part, not his. He is always standing with open arms waiting for my return.

Having experienced several years of depression,

alienation, and loneliness, I am very concerned that this not all sound like answers which are too simplistic. I remember so well how much it bothered me in my difficult times for someone to give me a simplistic, puritanical answer like, "You should try God."

My immediate reaction was always, "You obviously have never been where I am."

This is the reason I began chapter 4 to give suggestions for converting our loneliness into a solitude which could be used to establish a closer relationship with God. Then I used chapter 5 to try to show that, as Christians, we are not immune to trials and suffering but that God will help us to use these to prepare us for meeting the needs of the wounded all about us.

With all of this in mind, I have been trying to show how our faith can help us transcend many of the basic causes of loneliness.

It won't come all at once. Things of faith never do. When I see people becoming discouraged because they are comparing themselves to others and their rate of growth, their attitudes, their patience, I often feel for the twelve disciples. Look what they had to compare themselves to—the Lord himself, walking beside them! When they saw all that he accomplished through his faith they begged him, "Increase our faith" (Luke 17:5).

Jesus' answer to them was, "If you had faith as a grain of mustard seed, you could say to this sycamine tree, 'Be rooted up, and be planted in the sea,' and it would obey you" (Luke 17:6, RSV).

He was saying to them, "Use what you have. Use it today! Don't sit around and philosophize about how good it would be if you had more. The only way faith grows is by use, otherwise it is lost."

In the same way he says to us everyday, "Take what little faith you can muster today and go out and use it. You will see! Tomorrow you will have more!"

Each day we must trust his purpose, trust his presence, trust his power. Then each day there will be revealed to us how the things which may have appeared losses to us—suffering, weaknesses, loneliness, failures—can become the very things he will use to gain entrance for us into the life of someone he wants to bless through us. People in the midst of trials often find it hard to open up and take help from a perfect person who admits no failures. They are waiting for wounded, fellow travelers like us.

Try to be patient with yourself and with others in the time it takes to master the art of trusting and waiting to turn loneliness and pain into solitude and joy. When we find a person who is able to face times of aloneness, of isolation, alienation, and yet not be made lonely by it, we can be sure of one thing: it is not the first time that person has walked alone. It takes time to master loneliness and that mastery only comes by being alone. In solitude we are able to find the inner strength to support us, the certainty of divine companionship to undergird us, and the challenge of a world of lonely people who wait for us to share their pain and show them the wonderful resources waiting for those who will claim them in their solitary walk.

Sometimes God decides to use the circumstances of our lives to write indelibly on our hearts his eternal truths and his invitation to us to find our rest in him. He did this for me in recent years during a difficult time of illness and of trying to learn to trust the now of his plan.

After we had returned from Japan, I had suffered through a long series of pain and stomach disorders when it was discovered I had five ulcers. We tried treating them with medication and diet over a period of time. Three responded to the treatment, but two only worsened. It was decided to remove half of my stomach in the area where they were located. They assured me they had cut the vegus nerve controlling the supply of acid to the stomach so I should not be bothered with the problem again.

For some time, all went well. Then the severe stomach pains returned. When I went for a series of X rays, I was told that I had two very severe ulcers that indicated immediate surgery to remove another large section of my stomach.

I decided to go to Dallas to a hospital where my doctor brother could oversee an examination and advise me if the diagnosis were confirmed. Sure enough, they reported that the tests showed two deep ulcers had nearly eaten through the wall of my stomach and needed immediate surgery.

It was early in a new semester at my elementary school, and I objected. I felt my first grade class was at a very critical time, just beginning to make some real progress, and I was loathe to subject them to a month of getting acquainted with a new teacher. I begged to wait until our spring break for surgery.

It was finally agreed that if I would go for regular checkups at a Nashville hospital during the interim, I could wait until the spring break for surgery if the condition did not worsen. You can be sure I did a lot of praying that spring.

By Easter vacation nothing had improved, but nothing seemed appreciably worse. Once again I begged for more time for my class. It was decided I should keep in touch with the Nashville hospital and come to Dallas for surgery two days after school was out in early June.

The last time I went for X rays the reports were discouraging. The doctors told me that the ulcers seemed to be draining both into the stomach and outside. They warned me about surgery. I was overweight. I was severely anemic and very tired. They wanted me to know I was not too good a surgical risk. Furthermore, they warned me, a colostomy might well have to be performed, and they could not promise I could continue my very active role as a first grade teacher. Surgery was scheduled in two weeks.

I was worried and a little depressed, but I had so much to do to finish up the school year that I scarcely knew which way to turn. Finally it began to dawn on me that I was acting as if I had no one to turn my problems over to.

I made time to go aside and spend some time with God. In that time of meditation I felt impressed to say to him, "OK, God. I turn it all over to you. If you want me to make it through the surgery, fine. If my task is already finished, fine. If I am to continue to teach school, fine. If you have some other plan, fine. All of this caught me a little off guard, Lord, but I know it didn't catch you off guard. You knew all of the time what was going to happen, just like you know what is going to happen when I get to Dallas. Thank you for taking charge."

That night I didn't wake up with stomach pains. In fact, every day I seemed to feel better. I told my brother on the phone that maybe I didn't need surgery.

He laughed and said it was amazing how many people decide they are feeling better just before the scheduled time arrives.

When I got to Dallas they said the surgery had been postponed one day. Although several doctors had seen inside my stomach on the previous visit, the surgeon they had secured had not been one of them. Although he had studied the X rays, he wanted to get the light in there again and be sure exactly what he was doing. And so the examination was conducted.

The night before surgery, of course, I was not allowed liquids and the "nothing at all by mouth" regimen was already being enforced. The nurses had come by and prepared me for the surgery to be done at seven the next morning. I was getting drowsy, and visiting hours were about over.

Then my door opened, and five doctors walked in and stood in a ring about my bed.

"Why do doctors always look so solemn?" I wondered.

"Mrs. Hollaway," the surgeon began. "There's been a change of plans."

My heart sank.

"We have no real explanation for what has happened," he said. "When we looked inside your stomach today we could find no trace at all of the ulcers. I called in the doctors who saw them before. They were very clear on your last X rays, but we could not even find a scar where they had been. The opening to your stomach, which we thought was so poor we were going to have to close it up and make a new one, has repaired itself. Even your anemia is gone. We have canceled the surgery. You may go home in the morning."

I have had no further trouble. I tell the story with humble thanksgiving but also with some feeling of caution.

This is not always the way God works. Sometimes, as in the case of my first surgery, he allows things to progress in their normal, painful fashion. But this time he chose to intervene. I think he did it in response to my faith to say to me in a way I could never forget, "You were right to turn the reins over to me. You can trust the now of my plan for you. You can rest on the eternal ground where I have placed you. I want you always to remember that you need never walk alone again, for the eternal God *is* your refuge and the everlasting arms *are* beneath you."